PURPLE ZONE

(A)	VISITOR CENTRE
(H)	CAR PARK
101	1940 DUNKIRK VETERANS' ASSOCIATION
107a	NORWEGIAN NAVY FLAGPOLES

ORANGE ZONE

(B)	THE CLOISTERS (LEADING TO)
(B)	THE MILLENNIUM CHAPEL OF PEACE AND FORGIVENESS
(B)	MARKET SQUARE & KNICK KNACKS (CHARITY SHOP)
202	THE BLIND VETERANS UK (ST DUNSTAN'S) PATHWAY
204	INTERNATIONAL MILITARY MUSIC SOCIETY
205	THE ARMY BENEVOLENT FUND – THE SOLDIERS' CHARITY
206	CHURCH LADS' & CHURCH GIRLS' BRIGADE
206a	THE BOYS' BRIGADE
207	THE EX-NATIONAL SERVICEMEN'S MEMORIAL
208	AUXILIARY TERRITORIAL SERVICE STATUE
209	LICHFIELD & DISTRICT GARDEN
210	THE LEONARD CHESHIRE AMPHITHEATRE
211	THE BEVIN BOYS MEMORIAL
212	THE 'Y' SERVICES MEMORIAL
212a	OPERATION MARKET GARDEN / MARKET GARDEN VETERANS' ASSOCIATION
212b	1ST AIRBORNE RECONNAISSANCE SQUADRON
212c	GLIDER PILOT REGIMENT
213	GENERAL POST OFFICE MEMORIAL GARDEN
214	THE FAULD EXPLOSION MEMORIAL
215	ROYAL AIR FORCE HALTON APPRENTICES MEMORIAL GARDEN
216	THE TREFOIL GUILD WILLOW SCULPTURES
217	BRITISH LIMBLESS EX-SERVICE MEN'S ASSOCIATION (BLESMA)
218	THE ROYAL ARTILLERY GARDEN
219	THE INNER WHEEL GROVE
220	AUXILIARY TERRITORIAL SERVICE / ACK ACK
221	STILLBIRTH AND NEONATAL DEATH CHARITY MEMORIAL (SANDS)
222	ROYAL AIR FORCE REGIMENT
223	FIRE AND RESCUE SERVICES
223	TWIN TOWERS MEMORIAL

ORANGE ZONE (CONTINUED)

224	WOMEN'S ROYAL ARMY CORPS
225	CIVIL DEFENCE
226	SUEZ VETERANS' ASSOCIATION
227	CHANGI LYCH GATE
(G)	THE FAR EAST PRISONERS OF WAR MEMORIAL BUILDING
228	THE SUMATRA RAILWAY
229	THE FAR EAST PRISONERS OF WAR GROVE
230	BURMA RAILWAY
231	WOMEN'S AUXILIARY SERVICE – THE CHINTHE WOMEN
231	THE HONG KONG VOLUNTEER DEFENCE CORPS
231a	ROYAL NORFOLK REGIMENT, SUFFOLK REGIMENT AND CAMBRIDGESHIRE REGIMENT MEMORIAL
232	BURMA STAR
232a	THE CHINDIT MEMORIAL
234	THE ROTARY RIDGE
235	BRITISH KOREAN VETERANS ASSOCIATION
236	17TH DOGRA REGIMENT
236	BRIGADE OF GURKHAS
237	MALAYA AND BORNEO VETERANS MEMORIAL
238	ROYAL MALAYSIA POLICE
239	MALAYAN VOLUNTEER FORCE
240	SULTAN OF OMAN'S ARMED FORCES MEMORIAL
241	BALUCH REGIMENT

GREEN ZONE

(C)	ARMED FORCES MEMORIAL
301	NORMANDY VETERANS
302	KING'S AFRICAN RIFLES
303	THE ROYAL ENGINEERS
304	THE FREEMASONS
305	THE BEAT (POLICE MEMORIAL AVENUE)
305	SPECIAL CONSTABULARY
306	POLICE MEMORIAL GARDEN
307	THE POLAR BEAR MEMORIAL
308	BROTHERHOOD OF GREEK VETERANS CHAPEL
309	CAVALRY GROVE (CRESCENT)
310	THE PHANTOM MEMORIAL
311	THE ARMY PARADE
311a	THE ROYAL GREEN JACKETS
311b	10TH ROYAL HUSSARS

311c	YORKSHIRE
312	WAR WIDOWS' WOOD AND MEMORIAL
313	MEDITERRANEAN CAMPAIGNS OF WORLD WAR II
313	THE ROYAL HAMPSHIRE REGIMENT
313	GARDEN OF THE INNOCENTS
313	THE WAR WIDOWS' ROSE GARDEN
313a	THE ARMY WOOD
313b	ARMY AIR CORPS
314	ROYAL LOGISTIC CORPS
315	KENYA POLICE
316	ROYAL MILITARY POLICE ASSOCIATION
317	SOROPTIMIST INTERNATIONAL
318	BRITISH GERMAN FRIENDSHIP GARDEN
319	ANGLO-JAPANESE PEACE GARDEN
320	CELEBRATION OF LIFE GROVE
321	IRAQ / AFGHANISTAN WILLOWS
321a	BASRA MEMORIAL WALL
322	THE NAVY WOOD
323	THE BLUES AND ROYALS
324	ROYAL TANK REGIMENT
325	MERCIAN WOOD
325a	ROYAL CORPS OF SIGNALS
326	IRISH INFANTRY GROVE
327	COMMANDER DAVID CHILDS' TREES
327	THE GOLDEN GROVE
327	THE QUEEN ALEXANDRA'S ROYAL ARMY NURSING CORPS
327a	POLISH FORCES WAR MEMORIAL (E)
328	ROYAL ARMY MEDICAL CORPS
328	ROYAL ARMY DENTAL CORPS
329	SHOT AT DAWN (D)
330	LICHFIELD WOOD
330	ROYAL GLOUCESTERSHIRE, BERKSHIRE AND WILTSHIRE REGIMENT
330a	THE SHOWMEN'S GUILD OF GREAT BRITAIN
331	THE INTELLIGENCE CORPS
331	KINGFISHER WOOD
331	BIRMINGHAM CHILDREN'S HOSPITAL
331	GCHQ MEMORIAL
331a	ARMY APPRENTICE NATIONAL MEMORIAL

332	HOUSEHOLD DIVISION
332	LIGHT INFANTRY MEMORIAL
332	THE DURHAM LIGHT INFANTRY
332	THE MALL
332	1ST THE QUEEN'S DRAGOON GUARDS
332	THE PARACHUTE REGIMENT AND AIRBORNE FORCES
332	ROYAL ELECTRICAL AND MECHANICAL ENGINEERS (REME)
333	ROYAL AIR FORCE WOOD
334	ROYAL AIR FORCE CRANWELL APPRENTICES
335	ROYAL AIR FORCE BOY ENTRANTS
336	COASTAL COMMAND
336	RAF LOCKING
336	THE RAIL INDUSTRY
336	THE GIRLS VENTURE CORPS
336	RAF ADMINISTRATIVE APPRENTICES
336	THE CHELTENHAM COLLEGE MEMORIAL
337	WOMEN'S SECTION, THE ROYAL BRITISH LEGION
337	ROYAL NATIONAL LIFEBOAT INSTITUTION
337a	SHACKLETON ASSOCIATION MEMORIAL
338	THE 41 CLUB
339	ANCIENT BURIAL MOUND
340	THE ROYAL OBSERVER CORPS
340	II (ARMY COOPERATION) SQUADRON
340	RAF BENEVOLENT FUND
340a	ROYAL AIR FORCES ASSOCIATION REMEMBRANCE GARDEN
341	ROYAL & SUN ALLIANCE MEMORIALS
341a	NO 30 SQUADRON ASSOCIATION
342	ROYAL AIR FORCE SERVICING COMMANDO AND TACTICAL SUPPLY WING ASSOCIATION
343	ROYAL AUXILIARY AIR FORCE
343a	AIRCREW ASSOCIATION MEMORIAL
344	ROYAL CANADIAN AIR FORCE
344	ROYAL AIR FORCE WING
344a	THE ROYAL AIR FORCE POLICE
345	WOMEN'S AUXILIARY AIR FORCE (WAAF)
346	AIR FORMATION AND AIR SUPPORT SIGNALS

346a	90 SIGNALS UNIT
347	ROYAL AUSTRALIAN AIR FORCE
348	ADJUTANT GENERAL'S CORPS COMMEMORATIVE GARDEN
349	STAFFORDSHIRE REGIMENT
350	ASSOCIATION OF JEWISH EX-SERVICEMEN AND WOMEN
350a	THE SHRIEVALTY AVENUE
351	GALLIPOLI
352	MERCIAN VOLUNTEERS
353	HOME SERVICE FORCE
354	TOC H

BLUE ZONE

401	YEOMANRY AVENUE
401a	BRITISH SOUTH AFRICA POLICE
401b	NYASALAND POLICE MEMORIAL
402	ROYAL HONG KONG POLICE
402a	NORTHERN RHODESIA POLICE MEMORIAL
403	BIDADARI CEMETERY
403a	MEMORIAL FOR ST JOHN VOLUNTEERS
404	BLESMA EXTENSION
405	YANGTZE INCIDENT
406	ROYAL INDIAN NAVY AND INDIAN ARMY
407	FAR EAST AIR FORCE
408	DIAMOND GROVE
409	ROYAL NORWEGIAN NAVY
409a	NATIONAL ASSOCIATION OF MEMORIAL MASONS
410	FLEET AIR ARM
410a	ROYAL MARINES ASSOCIATION
411	BRITISH NUCLEAR TEST VETERANS
411a	THE COMMANDOS
411b	SHROPSHIRE YEOMANRY MEMORIAL PLINTH
411b	STAFFORDSHIRE YEOMANRY
412	SOUTH ATLANTIC MEDAL ASSOCIATION MEMORIAL AND THE ANTELOPE GARDEN
413	ROYAL NAVAL REVIEW
413a	ROYAL NAVAL PATROL SERVICE
414	DEFENSIVELY EQUIPPED MERCHANT SHIPS
415	MASTER MARINERS SUNDIAL
416	THE MERCHANT NAVY CONVOY WOOD
416	THE MERCHANT NAVY ASSOCIATION MEMORIAL
416a	ROYAL FLEET AUXILIARY SHIP 'SIR PERCIVALE' ANCHOR

417	WOMEN'S ROYAL NAVAL SERVICE
417	THE VOLUNTARY AID DETACHMENT (RN)
417	HMS BARHAM
417	RUSSIAN CONVOY VETERANS
417a	ARMY DOG UNIT (NORTHERN IRELAND) ASSOCIATION RED PAW
417b	THE QUEEN ALEXANDRA'S ROYAL NAVAL NURSING SERVICE AND THE VOLUNTARY AID DETACHMEET (RN)
418	ULSTER SPECIAL CONSTABULARY
418a	THE ROYAL BRITISH LEGION NEVER FORGET TRIBUTE GARDEN
419	ARMED SERVICES WOOD
419	LIONS CLUB INTERNATIONAL – WOODEN SHELTER
419a	DOUGLAS SKENE GROVE
420	THE ULSTER ASH GROVE
420	THE ULSTER DEFENCE REGIMENT CGC
420a	THE RUC GC WAY
421	THE HOME FRONT
421a	THE NATIONAL EX-PRISONER OF WAR ASSOCIATION
422	THE CHILDREN'S WOODLAND / ACTIVITY AREA
422a	THE EDWARD'S TRUST GARDEN
423	FELLOWSHIP OF THE SERVICES
424	MILLENNIUM WOOD
424a	WOMEN'S INSTITUTE
424a	THE SALVATION ARMY
424a	YMCA
424a	COMBINED OPERATIONS COMMAND MEMORIAL
425	THE ROYAL BRITISH LEGION POPPY FIELD
425a	THE SPIRITUALISTS' NATIONAL UNION
425b	QUAKER SERVICES MEMORIAL
426	RAC FUTURE FORESTS
427	THE ROADPEACE WOOD
428	ALLIED SPECIAL FORCES ASSOCIATION GROVE
429	WESTERN FRONT ASSOCIATION MEMORIAL
430	UNITED NATIONS AVENUE
430	THE FORESTERS FRIENDLY SOCIETY
431	WATERSMEET

CONTENTS

Content	Pg
ABOUT US	1 - 2
A RECLAIMED SITE	3 - 4
TREES	5 - 6
WILDLIFE	7 - 8
THE ARMED FORCES MEMORIAL	9 - 12
THE MILLENNIUM CHAPEL OF PEACE AND FORGIVENESS	13 - 16

Content	Pg
PURPLE ZONE	17 - 22
ORANGE ZONE	23 - 62
GREEN ZONE	63 - 124
BLUE ZONE	125 - 166
SUPPORTING THE ARBORETUM AND DONATIONS	167 - 168
DONATION FORM	169
ALPHABETICAL MEMORIAL INDEX	171 - 175

Photo by Sue Elliot

The National Memorial Arboretum is the UK's year-round Centre of Remembrance; a spiritually uplifting place which honours the fallen, recognises service and sacrifice, and fosters pride in our country.

Our vision is to create a world-renowned Remembrance Centre worthy of those who give so much to our country.

Where our Nation remembers

ABOUT US

The origins of the Arboretum can be traced back to a visit to Arlington Cemetery and the National Arboretum in Washington, DC, in 1988 by founder David Childs. He had the idea that such concepts could be introduced to the UK to provide a meaningful memorial to those who have served. David Childs was greatly supported by Group Captain Sir Leonard Cheshire VC OM DSO & 2 bars, DFC, who was concerned about future Remembrance and became influential in the concept of the Arboretum. The amphitheatre at the Arboretum is dedicated to his memory.

The then Prime Minister John Major launched the appeal to create the Arboretum in November 1994. At this stage there was no land or money for the project but this quickly changed when Redland Aggregates (now Lafarge Tarmac) generously gifted 82 acres of reclaimed gravel, working alongside the banks of the River Tame. This generous gift has now been extended by a further 70 acres, which includes the island in the River Tame.

The Arboretum was officially opened by HRH The Duchess of Kent on 16 May 2001.

The design was carefully conceived to provide both a space for peaceful contemplation and a living and growing environment for an assortment of trees and wildlife. Family members, friends and comrades can come and remember loved ones in a tranquil setting.

Located in the heart of the nation, with over 40,000 maturing trees (many of which are dedicated) and over 300 significant memorials, the National Memorial Arboretum is a beautiful and lasting tribute to those who served their country or who have died in conflict.

Photo by Barry Turner

A RECLAIMED SITE

265 million years ago, central England was part of a vast hot landscape of shallow lakes in red sandy desert. These conditions produced the red marl that forms the local 'bedrock' and gives the soil its distinctive red colour.

Millions of years later, during the Ice Age, a drop in temperature led to the breaking up and grinding together of rocks by frost action, which is the repeated freezing and thawing of water in rock. During warmer periods, meltwater rivers carried gravels from higher land to form the mineral deposits that are worked for aggregates today.

At the end of the Ice Age, thin layers of finely grained sediment were deposited over the gravels to form the soils which enabled plants to grow and farming to take place.

The sand and gravel, deposited in the Alrewas area thousands of years ago, is quarried by Lafarge Tarmac for use in construction throughout the region, including homes, schools, hospitals and roads. The land where the National Memorial Arboretum has been established was quarried in the late 1980s and early 1990s.

When the first phase of quarrying ceased, the land was restored using inert wastes, such as soils and clays, which cannot be recycled. The Arboretum's many groves have been established on this land.

Lafarge Tarmac will continue to quarry at Alrewas until the work is finished, and will restore the land progressively. The company is proud to have played a part in the development of the Arboretum and surrounding countryside.

In October 2002, the skull of a 40,000 year old woolly rhino was found in Lafarge Tarmac's Alrewas Quarry by digger driver Ray Davis. The woolly rhino lived during the middle part of the last major glaciation of the British region, about 30,000 to 60,000 years ago. Other finds at the quarry include remains of woolly mammoth, horse, bison and reindeer. Quarrying is important to archaeologists, who can quickly search for historical artefacts in large areas of land that are being quarried.

Photo by Lafarge Aggregates

TREES

Visitors to the National Memorial Arboretum can enjoy a wide variety of trees, many of which have a relevance to the memorials around them. Although still a 'young' Arboretum, there are already in excess of 40,000 trees in the grounds which are rapidly growing into a unique living tribute.

For example, The Beat is an avenue of London plane and chestnut trees which were funded by every Police Force in the UK. Chestnuts were chosen because the first truncheons were made from this extremely durable wood.

Visitors to the Chapel will be struck by the twelve pillars of Douglas fir. Construction of the Chapel began in 1999, the 200th anniversary of the birth of Scottish plant collector David Douglas. Between 1825 and 1827, Douglas travelled a staggering 10,000 miles in Western Canada and North West USA, on foot and by canoe, collecting and classifying plants. As a result of his efforts, 200 new plants were introduced to the UK, including the Douglas fir.

Three Dawn redwoods, Metasequoia glyptostrobides, can be found near the Railway Industry memorial, adjacent to the river bank. These magnificent trees, identified as a 'living fossil' in 1941, once blanketed the entire Northern Hemisphere and were thought to be extinct by Western botanists until their rediscovery in 1941 in the Sichuan Province of China. They also form the longest tree avenue in the world at 47km, approaching the city of Pizhou in China.

At the end of The Beat can be found the Golden Grove which celebrates the lives of couples who married at the end of World War II and commemorated their 50th anniversary by dedicating trees. All the trees in the Grove have golden leaves, fruits or stems such as the golden stemmed ash. At its centre is the magnificent Polish Armed Forces memorial.

Passing through the Golden Grove you will come across a sinuous line of young redwoods planted by the International Tree Foundation. During the California Gold Rush in the 1850s, a prospector searching for gold stumbled into a grove of giant redwood trees, Sequoiadendron giganteum. These are the world's largest trees in terms of volume. The General Sherman Tree in Sequoia National Park, California, is nearly 84 metres high, with the first branch 40 metres above ground level, it weighs around 2,100 tonnes. One day, we hope, our trees will be this big!

All of the hardy native tree species found in the UK, such as the black poplar and wild service tree, can be found at the Arboretum. The growing collection of temperate region trees, especially the North American oaks, will add a wide variety of autumn colour to the grounds.

EXPLORE THE WORLD OF TREES

A partnership has been created between the National Memorial Arboretum and Bedgebury Pinetum, Kent, which has the largest and most complete collection of temperate conifers in the world.

In 2009, forest fires in Greece burned 21,000 hectares of pine forest in just four days. One of the species we have been given is Abies cephalonica, the Grecian fir, a species devastated by the fire. When our trees are big enough to produce cones we will be able to offer seed / seedlings for restocking areas of Greece where the species has been lost.

Another example, the Serbian spruce, Picea ormorika, is extremely rare in the wild and endemic to only one valley in western Serbia. Should this population be lost, then arboreta like Bedgebury and the National Memorial Arboretum will be the only sites where there are specimens grown from wild-sourced seed. These could, if required, be used to help repopulate the Balkan forests. The trees we have planted have another role in educating people in the fields of arboriculture, conservation and environmental understanding.

EXAMPLE OF A BOTANIC LABEL

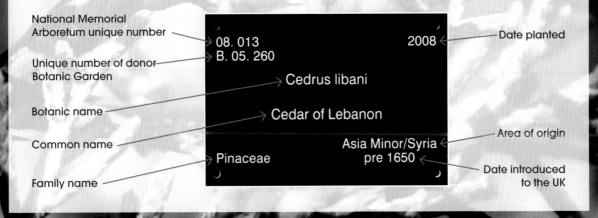

National Memorial Arboretum unique number → 08. 013

Unique number of donor Botanic Garden → B. 05. 260

2008 ← Date planted

Cedrus libani

Botanic name → Cedrus libani

Common name → Cedar of Lebanon

Asia Minor/Syria ← Area of origin

Pinaceae

Family name → Pinaceae

pre 1650 ← Date introduced to the UK

Photo by Barry Turner

Where our Nation remembers

WILDLIFE INFORMATION

The mix of habitats found in the Arboretum gives rise to an excellent home for a diversity of wildlife.

A variety of common species of birds have been seen, together with the following: blackcap, chiffchaff, goldeneye, hobby, kingfisher, little owl, oystercatcher, reed bunting and tufted duck. Rare birds have included a hoopoe and a black redstart. A dedicated bird feeding area is established within the Arboretum and we run at least two bird watching walks per year.

Other wildlife at the Arboretum includes foxes, badgers, brown hares, wood mice, bank voles, shrews, weasels, stoats, pipistrelles and Daubenton's bats.

Rabbits, otters, and mink have all been seen. The sighting of a hare by visitors is always a special event and surveys have found evidence of otters. Mammal surveys have been carried out and these are very popular with all visitors, providing the opportunity to see and touch live creatures. Similarly, bat walks by the River Tame at dusk are popular, with the use of bat detectors.

Other wildlife identified by the Environment Agency includes eel, roach, perch, chub and pike as well as many species of moths, butterflies, damselflies, and dragonflies. The attractive blue banded demoiselle damselfly is particularly numerous along the river banks during the summer months.

Pond dipping sessions by children have shown a great variety of pond life, including pond skaters, water boatmen, tadpoles, diving beetles and dragonfly nymphs.

We have several areas where wildflowers flourish – notably The Royal British Legion Poppy field, the riverside areas and the Bronze Age Burial Mound.

G Map reference

ARMED FORCES MEMORIAL

WHY THE MEMORIAL IS SO IMPORTANT

The service men and women of the British Armed Forces who have been killed whilst on duty, died in operational theatre or been targeted by terrorists since the end of World War II, are remembered here. Unlike the war memorials in towns and villages across the nation, there is nowhere else that records over 16,000 names of those who have been killed on duty in recent times.

Since 1948, the men and women of the Armed Forces have taken part in more than 50 operations and conflicts across the world, often as part of United Nations, NATO or other international coalitions. These actions have ranged from hot war to peacekeeping; from humanitarian assistance to fighting terrorism; from the jungles of Malaysia to the storms of the South Atlantic; from the seaport of Aden to the streets of Northern Ireland.

It is not just service men and women who have made sacrifices. Behind every name on the Memorial there are the wives, husbands, partners, parents, children and colleagues who loved them and who live with the pain and consequences of their loss every day.

THE MEMORIAL

The Armed Forces Memorial, dedicated in the presence of Her Majesty The Queen on 12 October 2007, is a nationally significant focus for Remembrance, providing recognition and thanks for those who have given their lives in the service of the country since the end of World War II.

The Memorial is a stunning piece of architecture designed by Liam O'Connor, which draws its inspiration from the ancient landscapes of prehistoric Britain and the classical forms of ancient Rome. It consists of a six metre high earth mound, 100 metres wide at the base reducing to just 50 metres wide at the top, which is based on early British barrows or tumuli. The spiral walkway up the grassy, tree-planted slopes provides accessibility to people of all ages and levels of mobility. At the top of the mound stands a 43 metre diameter stone structure, comprising two curved walls and two straight walls which are constructed of 200,000 bricks faced with over 1,000 tonnes of Portland stone panels. In recognition of the importance of Armistice Day, a gap has been left in the two southern walls, which allows a shaft of sunlight to penetrate to the heart of the Memorial, onto the central bronze wreath, on the eleventh hour of the eleventh day of the eleventh month of the year.

The Memorial is particularly important for the many families and friends who have no grave to visit, or who remember those in graves in far-off places. The Memorial plays a valuable role in helping all who grieve for a service person to come to terms with their loss, by providing a focus for their grief as they pass through different stages of their lives.

THE SCULPTURES

At the centre of the Memorial are two bronze sculptures, the embodiment of loss and sacrifice. Created by Ian Rank-Broadley, best known for his image of HM Queen Elizabeth II which has appeared on all UK and Commonwealth coinage since 1998, the sculptures bear silent witness to the cost of armed conflict. This significant work is becoming an icon identifiable to all and especially to those who live with the consequences of the nation's call to duty.

HOW THE NAMES ARE RECORDED

The names of those who have died are recorded first of all by year, within each year by Service – Royal Navy, Army, Royal Air Force – and then in date order, so colleagues who died in the same incident are grouped together. Naming starts on the left circular wall as you enter the Memorial from the steps.

To help you find a name quickly, you can look up the location of a relative or loved one by asking a member of our team at Reception. Every effort will be made to assist you with any queries.

The theatres of conflict where the United Kingdom Armed Forces have served since World War II include:

- Palestine 1945 – 1948
- Malaya 1948 – 1960
- Yangtze 1949
- Korea 1950 – 1953
- Canal Zone 1951 – 1954
- Kenya 1952 – 1956
- Cyprus 1955 – 1959
- Suez 1956
- Arabian Peninsula 1957 – 1960
- Congo 1960 – 1964
- Brunei 1962 – 1964
- Borneo 1962 – 1966
- Cyprus 1964 to present day
- Radfan 1964
- South Arabia 1964 – 1967
- Malay Peninsula 1964 – 1965
- Northern Ireland 1969 – 2007
- Dhofar 1969 – 1976
- Rhodesia 1979 – 1980
- South Atlantic 1982

- Lebanon 1983 – 1984
- Gulf of Suez 1984
- Gulf 1986 – 1989
- Peshawar 1989 – 1990
- Namibia 1989 – 1990
- Gulf 1990 – 1991
- Kuwait 1991
- Iraq / Kuwait 1991 – 2003
- Western Sahara 1991 to present day
- Northern Iraq / Southern Turkey 1991
- Iraq 1991 – 2003
- Cambodia 1991 – 1993
- Former Yugoslavia 1992 – 2002
- Sarajevo 1992 – 1996
- Georgia 1993 to present day
- Rwanda 1993 – 1996
- Angola 1995 – 1997
- Croatia 1996 – 1998

- Sierra Leone 1998 to present day
- Bosnia and Herzegovina 1996 to present day
- Kosovo 1998 – 2002
- Sierra Leone 1999 – 2002
- Congo 1999 to present day
- Kosovo 1999 to present day
- East Timor 1999
- Ethiopia and Eritrea 2000 to present day
- Macedonia 2001 – 2002
- Afghanistan 2001 to present day
- Balkans 2003 to present day
- Iraq 2003 – 2011
- Libya 2011

THE MILLENNIUM CHAPEL OF PEACE AND FORGIVENESS

The Chapel welcomes all people from all faiths and walks of life. It is the spiritual hub of the Arboretum.

The Chapel's wood construction is supported on twelve trunks of Douglas fir, each one representing one of the twelve apostles, carved by Jim Heath, on whose witness the early church was built.

The Chapel has no cornerstone, reflecting the idea that "Christ is our cornerstone".

THE MILLENNIUM PRAYER

The origins of the Chapel can be found in the desire to explore the true meaning of the Millennium. This also prompted Lord Lloyd Webber to run a competition to create a prayer for the Millennium. The winning prayer was written by 13 year-old Anna Crompton, from Ipswich. It is fitting that this prayer is now displayed on the front of the building to greet all our visitors. The carving was executed by Tom Staddon in cherry wood.

THE CANDLESTICKS

The altar candlesticks were created by a local partnership between Arthur Price, the internationally reputed tableware company, and Robert Carr, a Lichfield jeweller.

These represent the twelve knives of the apostles. They are bound by barbed wire as a reminder that people still starve as a result of war and imprisonment.

THE ALTAR CROSS

The cross of oak and burr walnut was designed and created by Daniel Lacey of Buckinghamshire and donated by Barbara Roberts.

THE CRUCIFIXION

The central cross has a copy of the Sword of Sacrifice, which is found in some CWGC cemeteries around the world.

THE ALTAR

In keeping with the spirit of the Chapel, the young offenders in Swinfen Hall Prison were invited to make the altar, lectern and pulpit. On the altar are carved two texts:

"When I was in prison ye visited me" and "Thy Father that seest in secret will reward thee openly"

THE ALTAR CLOTH AND LECTERN AND PULPIT FRONTALS

The altar cloth was commissioned by The Women's Section of The Royal British Legion with a design based on the theme taken from Revelations.

THE CAVENDISH CROSS

The large lime wood cross mounted on the wall opposite the altar was carved by Ken Willoughby of the Essex Woodcarvers as a tribute to the life and work of Baroness (Sue) Ryder of Warsaw CMG and Group Captain Sir Leonard Cheshire VC OM DSO & two Bars, DFC.

It is based on a processional cross in St Mary's Church, Cavendish, Suffolk.

THE TWO MINUTE SILENCE

From its first conception, it was felt that the Chapel should be the one place in the United Kingdom where the One Minute Silence was observed every day of the year.

To achieve this, an introduction to the Silence was recorded together with the Last Post and Reveille by the buglers of the Royal Marines. By combining these three elements, we formed the Two Minute Silence.

At 11 o'clock every day, a light shines onto the altar from the bearing and elevation of the sun at 11am on 11 November, Armistice Day. All those in the Chapel or amphitheatre at that time are invited to stop in silence and recall those who have lost their lives in conflict.

DEDICATION

The Chapel was dedicated by The Right Reverend Keith Sutton, the then Bishop of Lichfield, on 2 November 2000, All Souls Day.

THE STORYTELLER

This wonderful wooden carving on the east side of the Chapel was carved by the Essex Woodcarvers.

This work symbolises the link between the apostles represented on the pillars and the teachings of Christ today. The twelve young figures listening to the Storyteller each have the potential to become new apostles of the holy word. The children who modelled for the work are all friends of the carvers while the model for Christ himself was their local vicar.

Photo by Barry Turne

THE PURPLE ZONE

Access: These memorials are accessible from the car park and entrance area to the Visitor Centre.

Terrain: Mostly firm surface suitable for all abilities.

Starting point: Main entrance gate.

No	Memorial	Pg
Ⓐ	VISITOR CENTRE	
Ⓗ	CAR PARK	
101	1940 DUNKIRK VETERANS' ASSOCIATION	21
107a	NORWEGIAN NAVY FLAGPOLES	22

"THE SITE CAN LOOK FORWARD TO A VERY
LONG, HEALTHY AND MUCH VISITED FUTURE.
WE HOPE THAT YOU ENJOY YOUR VISIT AND
TAKE MANY THOUGHTS AWAY WITH YOU."
David Childs, founder of the National Memorial Arboretum.

1940 DUNKIRK VETERANS' ASSOCIATION

The avenue of poplar trees, the seats and memorial plinth surrounded by sand brought from the beaches of Dunkirk was dedicated on 26 September 1999. The custom of using a rifle, boots, helmet and bayonet to mark a grave was used extensively during the American Civil War. During World War II, this custom was continued to mark the graves of fallen soldiers so that the bodies could be recovered later. The rifle topped with a helmet has become known as the Battlefield Cross or Fallen Soldier's Cross.

The memorial is a living tribute to all who took part in the operation code-named 'Dynamo', the evacuation of the Allied Armies from Dunkirk and neighbouring beaches between 26 May and 4 June 1940. During the course of the operation some 338,000 troops reached safety in England after being evacuated from Dunkirk and from beaches stretching 10 miles eastwards from the entrance to Dunkirk harbour. This evacuation was carried out by Royal Navy and Merchant Navy ships, aided by Allied ships and a mixed fleet of 'little ships'.

Photo by Barry Turner

Photo by Barry Turner

Photo by By Phil Nixon

107a

NORWEGIAN NAVY FLAGPOLES

Standing to the right of the front entrance to the Visitor Centre are three flagpoles which were donated by the Norwegian Navy.

The Silver Birch trees, pictured, form part of the Royal Norwegian Navy Memorial.

THE ORANGE ZONE

Access: From the Long Gallery in the Visitor Centre.

Terrain: Mostly firm surface suitable for all abilities.

Starting point: Cloister Walkway.

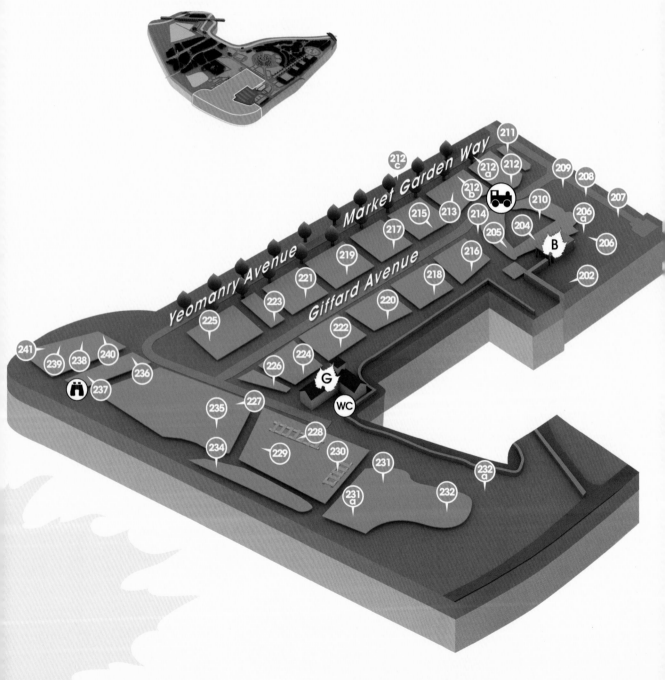

No	Memorial	Pg
Ⓑ	THE CLOISTERS (LEADING TO)	27
Ⓑ	THE MILLENNIUM CHAPEL OF PEACE AND FORGIVENESS	13
Ⓑ	MARKET SQUARE & KNICK KNACKS (CHARITY SHOP)	
202	THE BLIND VETERANS UK (ST DUNSTAN'S) PATHWAY	28
204	INTERNATIONAL MILITARY MUSIC SOCIETY	28
205	THE ARMY BENEVOLENT FUND – THE SOLDIERS' CHARITY	29
206	CHURCH LADS' & CHURCH GIRLS' BRIGADE	29
206a	THE BOYS' BRIGADE	30
207	THE EX-NATIONAL SERVICEMEN'S MEMORIAL	30
208	AUXILIARY TERRITORIAL SERVICE STATUE	31
209	LICHFIELD & DISTRICT GARDEN	32
210	THE LEONARD CHESHIRE AMPHITHEATRE	32
211	THE BEVIN BOYS MEMORIAL	33
212	THE 'Y' SERVICES MEMORIAL	33
212a	OPERATION MARKET GARDEN / MARKET GARDEN VETERANS' ASSOCIATION	34
212b	1ST AIRBORNE RECONNAISSANCE SQUADRON	34
212c	GLIDER PILOT REGIMENT	35
213	GENERAL POST OFFICE MEMORIAL GARDEN	36
214	THE FAULD EXPLOSION MEMORIAL	37
215	ROYAL AIR FORCE HALTON APPRENTICES MEMORIAL GARDEN	37
216	THE TREFOIL GUILD WILLOW SCULPTURES	38
217	BRITISH LIMBLESS EX-SERVICE MEN'S ASSOCIATION (BLESMA)	38
218	THE ROYAL ARTILLERY GARDEN	39
219	THE INNER WHEEL GROVE	39
220	AUXILIARY TERRITORIAL SERVICE / ACK ACK	40
221	STILLBIRTH AND NEONATAL DEATH CHARITY MEMORIAL (SANDS)	41
222	ROYAL AIR FORCE REGIMENT	43
223	FIRE AND RESCUE SERVICES	43
223	TWIN TOWERS MEMORIAL	44

No	Memorial	Pg
224	WOMEN'S ROYAL ARMY CORPS	44
225	CIVIL DEFENCE	45
226	SUEZ VETERANS' ASSOCIATION	46
227	CHANGI LYCH GATE	47
Ⓖ	THE FAR EAST PRISONERS OF WAR MEMORIAL BUILDING	48
228	THE SUMATRA RAILWAY	49
229	THE FAR EAST PRISONERS OF WAR GROVE	51
230	BURMA RAILWAY	53
231	WOMEN'S AUXILIARY SERVICE – THE CHINTHE WOMEN	54
231	THE HONG KONG VOLUNTEER DEFENCE CORPS	55
231a	ROYAL NORFOLK REGIMENT, SUFFOLK REGIMENT AND CAMBRIDGESHIRE REGIMENT MEMORIAL	56
232	BURMA STAR	57
232a	THE CHINDIT MEMORIAL	58
234	THE ROTARY RIDGE	58
235	BRITISH KOREAN VETERANS ASSOCIATION	59
236	17TH DOGRA REGIMENT	59
236	BRIGADE OF GURKHAS	60
237	MALAYA AND BORNEO VETERANS MEMORIAL	60
238	ROYAL MALAYSIA POLICE	61
239	MALAYAN VOLUNTEER FORCE	61
240	SULTAN OF OMAN'S ARMED FORCES MEMORIAL	62
241	BALUCH REGIMENT	62

Ronald Searle
Singapore 1945

"SEEING WHAT HAS HAPPENED TO THESE MEN
AND WOMEN, WE MUST NEVER FORGET THE
SACRIFICES THEY HAVE MADE. A FITTING TRIBUTE
TO THOSE WHO SUFFERED – MAY WE NEVER FORGET
THEM ALL."

Taken from visitor comments book, FEPOW memorial building.

After working on the Thai-Burma railway, artist Ronald Searle (right) spent more than a year in Changi before liberation. He described his drawings as 'the graffiti of a condemned man who found himself among the reprieved.'

I was always terrified that the Kempei-tai – the Japanese equivalent of the (German) Gestapo – would stumble on my drawings. But they never did and my head stayed on my shoulders.

Sapper Ronald Searle, Royal Engineers

Photo by Barry Turner

THE CLOISTERS

THE ROSE GARDEN WALK

The paviours set between the plain bricks in the walkway around the Cloisters and Chapel are laid down in commemoration of an event or in memory of someone's life. The tributes are for individuals, clubs or associations, and friends, family or colleagues have sponsored them. The path in front of the Garden of the Innocents is also part of the paved walk.

THE MEMORIAL PLAQUES ON THE CLOISTER WALLS

The Insurance Company plaques are from Royal and Sun Alliance offices and commemorate personnel who lost their lives in the two World Wars. As offices were closed or relocated, the plaques were gathered together into a memorial garden at the company head office and, when this office was itself relocated, Royal and Sun Alliance asked for them to be installed in the Arboretum. There are also two freestanding memorials just off Millennium Avenue. The company continues to cover all maintenance costs and insurance fees.

The Shipping Line plaques are from P & O Shipping Line offices. As with the insurance company, P & O have relocated to new offices that do not provide suitable hanging space for the large plaques. P & O covered refurbishment and hanging costs in the Cloisters. The wooden plaque created by 'The Mouseman', Yorkshireman Robert Thompson, is an interesting and valuable one. Look for the woodcarver's well-known trademark mouse on the edge of the plaque.

There are also plaques remembering employees from the Vestey Group plc. The Vestey family, already importing foodstuffs from the United States of America, saw the need for chilled transport and created the Blue Star Line. This enabled them to import food, particularly beef, into the country from their own farms in South America and Australia. They expanded into the wholesale and retail business in the UK and are one of Britain's largest companies.

Other plaques include those from railway companies such as the London Midland & Scottish.

Photo by Barry Turner

Photo: copyright National Memorial Arboretum

202

THE BLIND VETERANS UK (ST DUNSTAN'S) PATHWAY

From the Chapel to Gifford Avenue. The scented pathway is lined with all-year-round fragrant shrubs.

204

INTERNATIONAL MILITARY MUSIC SOCIETY

The International Military Music Society (IMMS) was formed in the UK in 1977 to promote interest in military music and it now has branches worldwide.

The memorial consists of block paving to the front of the Chapel overlooking the amphitheatre, creating a stage for performances, and four plaques on the Chapel shutters, representing the Royal Marines Band Service, the Corps of Army Music, Royal Air Force Music Services and IMMS itself.

These plaques commemorate the incalculable number of bandsmen, drummers, pipers and buglers who lost their lives in the service of their country, and celebrate the courage and fortitude of those military musicians whose actions were recognised with awards for bravery.

Photo by OceanBarefoot*

THE ARMY BENEVOLENT FUND – THE SOLDIERS' CHARITY

The Army Benevolent Fund – The Soldiers' Charity (ABF) Memorial Rose Garden is the site of a number of tribute roses, all of which represent loved ones who have served or who were part of the extended Army family. Some are young soldiers who were killed in peacetime activities or in action in Afghanistan and Iraq. The Rose Fund Tribute Book is held in the Millennium Chapel. The name of the rose is "The Jubilee Rose".

In 2010, a new plinth was dedicated at the end of the rose bed.

Photo by Barry Turner

CHURCH LADS' AND CHURCH GIRLS' BRIGADE

The garden was one of the first memorials to be created after the Arboretum itself was opened to the general public. Also dedicated during the ceremony was the Lectern Bible which was donated by the Brigade Association for use in the Millennium Chapel in Advent 2001.

It is estimated that around 50,000 Brigade Lads served in World War I, during which many honours and distinctions were awarded, including 21 Victoria Crosses. It is not recorded how many Brigade personnel served in World War II, nor the honours awarded, but an additional Brigade lad received the VC in 1945 posthumously. Younger Brigade lads and girls also served on the Home Front in both world wars.

The 22 Berberis shrubs were selected to represent the Brigade's military past but, more specifically, to represent our 22 Victoria Cross recipients. The Pathways form a Christian Cross to represent the Brigade's present path. The two benches commemorate the 16th Battalion of the Kings Royal Rifle Corps which was comprised entirely of past and present members of the Brigade in World War I. This was known as a "Pals' Battalion."

THE BOYS' BRIGADE

This garden, a grass rectangle with one corner curved, is bounded by a low hedge of field maple and box. At the entrance, two pieces of 5,000 year old 'bog oak' donated by the Republic of Ireland and the Northern Ireland Districts depict the twin pillars of Religion and Discipline. A path winds down to a small patio area where visitors can sit on a bench, set on a bed of Portland stone.

A large granite rock from Scotland, to which a real metal anchor is attached and inscribed with the chorus of The Boys' Brigade Hymn "Will your anchor hold?", occupies a prominent position, as does a solid slate plinth from Wales in the centre of the patio.

500 bulbs were planted in 2009 – 125 bulbs each of standard daffodils, pheasant-eye narcissi, Tête-à-tête daffodils and blue grape hyacinths. The bulbs represent the 125 years of existence of The Boys' Brigade.

A time capsule was buried in the garden containing items from Boys' Brigade young people in 2009.

Photo by Barry Turner

Photo by Barry Turner

THE EX-NATIONAL SERVICEMEN'S MEMORIAL

The memorial is dedicated to all who served their country as National Service men between 1939 and 1962. The memorial sculpture, made of green granite, was designed by Ian Stewart and represents the four cardinal points of the compass where National Service was performed. The memorial sculpture, garden and seating were dedicated on National Service Day, 29 June 2003. A commemorative Ex-National Servicemen's service and parade is held annually on the last Sunday in June.

Photo by Barry Turner

208

AUXILIARY TERRITORIAL SERVICE STATUE

The life-size statue of an Auxiliary Territorial Service (ATS) girl wearing basic khaki uniform was sponsored by the Auxiliary Territorial Service as a tribute to their members who played an important role in World War II from 1939 to 1945. Made up of volunteers who undertook six weeks of basic training, the ATS was formed in September 1938. By December 1939 there were 23,900 women aged between 19 and 23 years old in the service, peaking in 1943 at 212,500.

In 1949, the ATS was disbanded and the Women's Royal Army Corps (WRAC) was formed. During hostilities, 335 members of the ATS were killed, 94 reported missing, 302 wounded and 20 became POWs. The statue is the work of Birmingham sculptor Andy De Comyn who used his wife Francesca as the model. It consists of a cementitious render over a reinforced concrete core. The appearance is similar to limestone and is designed to withstand weathering and acid rain.

Where our Nation remembers

LICHFIELD & DISTRICT GARDEN

Photo by Barry Turner

The seat with a canopy in the centre of the garden represents the three spires of Lichfield Cathedral. Arranged around the seat is a planting of trees, one for each parish within the Lichfield District.

The trees were sponsored by each parish and placed in the geographical position relative to Lichfield. Lichfield District Council sponsored the seating and garden.

THE LEONARD CHESHIRE AMPHITHEATRE

The amphitheatre located outside the Chapel is dedicated to the memory of Group Captain Sir Leonard Cheshire VC OM DSO & 2 bars, DFC, the founder of the eponymous homes and services, whose concerns for future Remembrance influenced the concept of the National Memorial Arboretum. Chapel services are occasionally relayed into the amphitheatre, concerts have been performed here and the 11am Act of Remembrance can be broadcast into the amphitheatre, when occasion arises. The copper beech trees planted at the far side were chosen because they were Lord Cheshire's favourite trees. HM The Queen and HRH Prince Philip planted the trees at each end of the Army Benevolent Fund rose bed outside the Chapel on 3 July 2002.

THE BELL

Located on the raised bank of the amphitheatre is a large brass bell donated by Les Wills MBE, one of the Arboretum's volunteers, in memory of his wife Betty who served in the Women's Royal Naval Service (WRNS). The Bell started life on one of the Bedford Fire Appliances that were in use in the City of Birmingham during 1960 / 70 and was presented to Les Wills QFSM by the personnel at A1 Central, Birmingham, on his retirement from the West Midlands Fire Service in 1987 as Assistant Chief Fire Officer (Operations).

The Bell now has a modern day purpose, similar to that of a 'curfew bell' in that it is rung daily, shortly before the Arboretum's closing time.

Photo by By Phil Nixon

THE BEVIN BOYS MEMORIAL

During World War II there was a shortage of skilled mine workers and between 1943 and 1948 nearly 48,000 young men known as the Bevin Boys, many of whom were conscripts, joined regular miners in their dirty, dangerous but essential work keeping the coal supplies flowing. If his National Registration number was drawn out, a conscript was sent down the mines. Life was hard and dangerous for these men and many lost their lives.

Famous Bevin Boys have included Eric Morecambe and Brian Rix, who left the RAF to join the Bevin Boys.

The Bevin Boys memorial is created in stone from a quarry near Kilkenney in Ireland, the rough surface of which resembles the natural dark grey colour of coal, especially when wet. On the upper surface of the smaller of the two blocks are carved the tools used by the miners in the 1940s. There are two mice hidden in the carvings as they were commonly found in coal mines. The three planted trees represent the regions in which the Bevin Boys served: narrow oak (England), mountain ash (Wales) and Scots pine (Scotland).

THE 'Y' SERVICES MEMORIAL

The paths in this garden are laid out to form the letter 'Y' with dedicated benches and memorials alongside.

Initially, the 'Y' Group were mainly women from the ATS, WRNS and WAAF who were given the title of Special Wireless Operators – the 'Y' originating from Wireless Intercept (Signals Intelligence). One of the main intercept stations during World War II was Beaumanor Hall. This station, along with other similar sites around the UK, intercepted German signals (mainly Morse code) which were then passed to Bletchley Park, known as Station X. Operators became very skilled at this task and were able to tell individual enemy operators by the way that they used their Morse keys, thus helping to track enemy unit movements. Historians have indicated that the work carried out by the Special Wireless Operators shortened World War II by two years. The veil of secrecy that had prevailed for several decades began to lift in the 1960s.

In the right hand corner of the garden is a bench dedicated to Able Seaman Colin Grazier and Lt. Tony Fasson, who were posthumously awarded the George Cross, and 16 year-old NAAFI assistant Tommy Brown, who was awarded the George Medal, for their part in capturing the code books and documents from U-559.

OPERATION MARKET GARDEN / MARKET GARDEN VETERANS' ASSOCIATION

Operation Market Garden was the code name for an Allied operation which took place in September 1944 to secure a series of bridges over the major rivers of the German-occupied Netherlands. 'Market' was the code name of the airborne assault and 'Garden' the ground assault. A memorial plinth and plaque tell the story of the assault and the orange plaque alongside remembers the Dutch Underground resistance and the assistance they gave the British and Allied troops during Market Garden.

The Market Garden Veterans' Association was formed to recognise the contribution of ground troops who had fought their way from Normandy through France, Belgium and into Holland. There is also an Airborne Association that celebrates Operation Market Garden every September in the Netherlands.

Photo by Barry Turner

1ST AIRBORNE RECONNAISSANCE SQUADRON

In 1941, The Army Council decided to set up the Reconnaissance Corps. By June 1942, every division of the British Army had its own reconnaissance regiment whose motto was "Only the enemy in front, every other beggar behind".

The small black Scottish granite memorial is dedicated to the men of the 1st Airborne Reconnaissance Squadron, known as the Freddie Gough Squadron.

GLIDER PILOT REGIMENT

The Regiment was established in 1942 and remained active until 1957, when it was absorbed into the modern Army Air Corps.

The Regiment's motto was "Nothing is impossible", as the nature of their one way trips required the aircrews to subsequently join in combat operations on the ground. The Regiment's highly trained aircrew was also used to great effect in covert activity.

In the post war years, the Regiment remained active, undertaking liaison and reconnaissance roles in the Light Aircraft Flights operated by the Army. On 1 September 1957, the Regiment disbanded to create the foundation of what was to become the modern Army Air Corps.

The memorial stone is sourced from Gelderland in the Netherlands to acknowledge the Regiment's major role in the Battle of Arnhem.

Photo by By Phil Nixon

GENERAL POST OFFICE MEMORIAL GARDEN

The renovation of this garden was carried out by volunteers from the Royal Mail Group (RMG). The path is laid out to replicate the Royal Mail insignia in the shape of a cruciform.

The EIIR boxes date from the years 1952 – 1991. The words 'Royal Mail' first appeared on a British pillar box in 1991, reflecting organisational changes in the business. All the boxes have the relevant sovereign crowns depicted.

The green Victorian wall box came into service between 1871 and 1901. The one on display was bomb-damaged during the blitz when it was blown out of a wall in Deptford, East London. The local people then rebuilt a wall around the box to keep it in service.

This memorial is a tribute to the thousands of employees who died or were wounded, to families who suffered, and to all Post Office people who worked steadfastly to keep services going through the turmoil and tragedy of war. Messages in letters, telegrams and telephone calls became vital lifelines for anxious relatives and friends at home and a medium of support to those on the battlefields. Also remembered are those who are still serving in the Territorial Armies around the world today.

Photo by OceanBarefoot

THE FAULD EXPLOSION MEMORIAL

In November 1944, an estimated 4,000 tons of bombs and ammunition stored in a Gypsum mine were accidentally detonated, killing seventy people, including army personnel, Italian Prisoners of War who were working in the ammunition factory and local residents and workers.

It is believed that this site remains the largest single explosion caused by conventional weapons in both war and peacetime.

The explosion crater is situated about half a mile to the east of The Cock Inn at Hanbury, Staffordshire, about twelve miles from the Arboretum. In 1990, having been donated by an Italian firm, a granite memorial to those who lost their lives was erected near the crater. The crater is clearly visible to walkers and visitors to the area, but its true depth of over 100ft has gradually been decreased as trees and other vegetation have grown as the years have gone by.

Photo by Barry Turner

ROYAL AIR FORCE HALTON APPRENTICES MEMORIAL GARDEN

The association between the Halton House estate in Buckinghamshire and the RAF began in autumn 1912, when forces from Aldershot needed somewhere to practise the defence of London using their three aircraft and an airship.

Today RAF Halton is a major RAF training establishment. The centrepiece of the garden represents the RAF Apprentice wheel badge. The tree to the left of the stone is dedicated to Thomas Gray, posthumously awarded the Victoria Cross in 1940 for coolness and resourcefulness while navigating the leading aircraft under most difficult conditions on a mission to destroy a bridge that was allowing German forces to cross into Belgium.

THE TREFOIL GUILD WILLOW SCULPTURES

The Trefoil Guild, a corporate member of Girl Guiding since 2007, was formed as far back as 1920 for ex-Guides who wished to continue supporting Guiding and meeting old friends.

Presently there are over 1,100 Guilds in the UK with a membership of over 20,000. Guilds support Guiding with starter packs for new units and financial help for Girl Guiding members working and travelling abroad. They enjoy social events of their own and give practical help to Guiding and Scouting and their own community.

The Royal Family has always been closely connected with Guiding. HM The Queen, now Girl Guiding's Patron, and the late Princess Margaret, became members in childhood. The late Queen Mother was Trefoil Guild Patron from 1960 until her death.

The willows in the garden have been planted and woven into the shape of the three leaves and stalk of the Trefoil, the badge of the Trefoil Guild and of Girl Guiding.

BRITISH LIMBLESS EX-SERVICE MEN'S ASSOCIATION (BLESMA)

BLESMA was formed by various groups of severely disabled amputees trying to adjust to life in the so-called "land fit for heroes" in the years just after World War I.

In 1932, they all came together and the Association was formed. The fellowship of shared experience and the desire to get things done and to get things changed has always driven the Association.

Today, BLESMA still supports many veterans who lost limbs in World War II and in conflicts thereafter, offering its special skills to a new generation of young men and women disabled in the service of our country. BLESMA's youngest member to date has been 19 years old – its oldest 99 years old.

The fruit trees are kept at a low height to allow the blossom to be smelled and the fruit to be picked from wheelchairs.

THE ROYAL ARTILLERY GARDEN

The Royal Artillery dates back to the eighteenth century and by the end of World War II had become larger than the Royal Navy. The modern RA uses a variety of equipment designed to fulfil a wide range of roles.

This pleasant garden, with its waterfall, range of planting and seats in the form of old gun carriages, owes its design and creation to the energies of Ray Hutchins, a local artist and former member of the Royal Artillery, and was created and subsequently maintained by Association members themselves. The alder tree planted on the island in the centre of the water feature is doubly significant, as alder charcoal was once used in the production of gunpowder and the name Alrewas is derived from 'alder wash', the alders in the river/wash. Around the garden and on the banking are trees dedicated to the Royal Artillery.

A few famous names are associated with the Royal Artillery:

- Spike Milligan (comedian)
- Orde Wingate (inspirational leader)
- Anthony Quayle (actor)
- Edward Heath (Prime Minister)
- E H Shepard (illustrator)
- Frankie Howerd (comedian)
- Sir Denis Thatcher (husband of a previous Prime Minister)

Photo by Barry Turner

THE INNER WHEEL GROVE

Inner Wheel was founded in Manchester in 1924. Its members are the female spouses, partners and relatives of Rotary International members. As the movement spread, International Inner Wheel was formed in 1967. Its aims are to promote true friendship, encourage the ideals of personal service and foster international understanding.

The design of the Grove is based on the Inner Wheel Badge and echoes the gold and blue cogwheels in the trees and shrubs. In autumn 2008, the entrance to the Grove was enhanced by the erection of wrought iron gates, which were dedicated in March 2009.

Photo by Barry Turner

AUXILIARY TERRITORIAL SERVICE / ACK ACK

It is fitting that the ladies who manned the anti-aircraft guns in World War II, the Auxiliary Territorial Service / ACK ACK (ATS / ACK ACK), who were members of the Royal Artillery, should have their garden next to the Royal Artillery. The driving force behind this garden was Mrs Vee Robinson, a veteran of the organisation.

She visited a quarry on several blasting days until she found the rock that is placed in the centre of the garden. The shape reminds us of the angle of the search lights and guns which the ATS / ACK ACK girls worked with, and there is a poem and dedication engraved on the back of the stone. The garden was dedicated on 28 July 2000 at a ceremony attended by Lady Soames, the daughter of Sir Winston Churchill. The garden includes red flowering Malus planted over blue shrubs, the colours of the RA, and the Leylandii 'Robinson's Gold' in one corner which is a tribute to Vee Robinson.

STILLBIRTH AND NEONATAL DEATH CHARITY MEMORIAL (SANDS)

The charity was formed in 1978. It was set up by a small group of bereaved parents devastated by the death of their babies and by a complete lack of acknowledgement and understanding of the significance and impact of their loss.

SANDS aims to support anyone affected by the death of a baby; to work with health professionals to improve the quality of care and services provided to bereaved parents and their families and to promote changes in antenatal practice and fund research that could help to reduce the loss of babies' lives.

The SANDS Garden was designed by Nicholas Newton to reflect the emotional journey that many parents face in trying to come to terms with their bereavement. At the heart of the garden is a sculpture of the SANDS tear drop insignia which was created by John Roberts and the Portland Sculpture Trust to encourage adults and children to sit and touch the central carved figure of the baby. Two benches individually carved by Nigel Ross from reclaimed elm have been placed nearby.

ROYAL AIR FORCE REGIMENT

The Royal Air Force (RAF) Regiment provides specialist Force Protection for military airbases worldwide and is a unique Corps within the RAF. It has been on operations constantly since World War II. HM The Queen is Air Commodore-in-Chief of the RAF Regiment.

The RAF Regiment was formed on the prompting of Sir Winston Churchill and by the Royal Warrant of His Majesty King George VI in 1942. However, its roots go back to the 1920s when the RAF Armoured Car Companies were formed to protect the RAF assets exercising Air Control in the Middle East. Since its inception, it has fought in every major conflict and operational theatre, gaining a world-renowned reputation for its professionalism and expertise.

The RAF Regiment's Memorial Garden was dedicated on 5 April 2001 and the stark but impressive black granite memorial stone commemorates the worldwide service and sacrifice of Corps members since 1942. The shape of the paved area represents a landing strip and the grouping of the four Prunus amanogawa in each corner represents the four corners of the world in which the Corps serves. The Corps motto is "Per Ardua"; translated it reads, "Through Adversity".

Photo by David Faul

FIRE AND RESCUE SERVICES

The monument, 'Fire-fighters Serving Humanity', is a six and a half ton block of red granite, surmounted by a stainless steel and enamel badge and engraved on both sides. It recognises the qualities of operational fire and rescue service personnel, past, present and future, who serve all the communities of our Nation.

The eight points or tenets of the star depicted on the monument represent the qualities required of a fire-fighter:

TACT – GALLANTRY – DEXTERITY – OBSERVATION – PERSEVERANCE – LOYALTY – EXPLICITNESS – SYMPATHY

TWIN TOWERS MEMORIAL

The memorial was dedicated on the first anniversary of the terrorist attack on the twin towers and commemorates those who lost their lives in the World Trade Centre in New York in 2001. The Memorial contains debris from 'Ground Zero' that has been entrusted to us by the British Fire and Rescue Services and was donated by their counterparts in the USA.

224

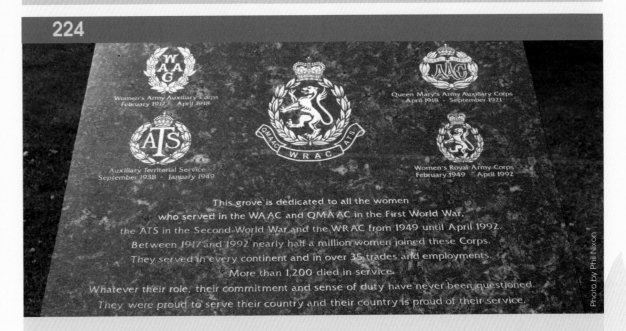

Photo by Phil Nixon

WOMEN'S ROYAL ARMY CORPS

The Women's Royal Army Corps (WRAC) and its predecessors, the Women's Army Auxiliary Corps, Queen Mary's Army Auxiliary Corps and the Auxiliary Territorial Service, are remembered here.

The front of the grove is based on the letter 'W' for women and behind is a more open area for seating and contemplation. The trees and shrubs planted were specially selected for their grace and elegance and also with three themes in mind: the bottle green of the WRAC uniform, the Corps Air "The Nut Brown Maid" and the connection with women's names.

Between 1917 and 1992, nearly half a million women joined the corps, serving in every continent in over 35 trades with more than 1,200 dying in service.

Photo by David Faul

CIVIL DEFENCE

The large central memorial stone commemorates the 1,900,000 who served in the Civil Defence Services during World War II and the nearly 7,000 who were killed. Their names and details are recorded in the Book of Remembrance lodged in the Chapel.

The smaller stone reminds us of the service given by animals, both those working and those simply helping to maintain the morale of their owners. The garden was dedicated in June 2001.

To the right of the path, towards the centre, is a tree (dedicated in 2007) and the memorial (dedicated in 2011), which includes a piece of rock from Gibraltar, to those who were awarded the George Cross for Civil Defence service.

At the far end is the memorial to the volunteer service (350,000 at any one time) given by the Civil Defence Corps and the Auxiliary Fire Service between 1949 and 1968 during the height of the Cold War. It was unveiled in 2008 by HRH The Duke of Gloucester.

SUEZ VETERANS' ASSOCIATION

The 16 October 1951 to 19 October 1954 period became known as the 'Emergency Period' when service personnel were deemed to be 'On Active Service'. This service was not recognised by the award of the General Service Medal until June 2003, some 50 years later, after a vigorous campaign.

Britain's Small Wars – Suez Canal Zone (1951 – 1954)

The Suez crisis of 1956 is often viewed as a major focus of post-war political history. Less well-known, certainly among the wider British public, were the years of conflict that preceded it. It was from those earlier years that the roots of the 'Suez Crisis' were sown in the towns and villages of the Suez Canal Zone in what became known as the 'Egyptian Emergency' of 1951 – 54.

The Canal Zone was known as 'the worst posting in the world' and the British Armed Forces (about a third of whom were RAF personnel) stationed there were mainly conscripts of National Service. The hostile climate, primitive sanitation, diseases and poor food all combined to make life very unpleasant. As if this was not enough, Egyptian terrorists began murderous attacks upon servicemen and their families, army camps, airfields and installations.

By the time the Anglo-Egyptian agreement ended the conflict in 1954, the number of post-war casualties accounted for some 1,400 lives. It took 50 years of campaigning before veterans finally received the Canal Zone Medal.

Photo by Phil Nixon

TO ALL WHO SERVED

Photo by Barry Turner

ERECTED BY 18ᵗʰ DIVISION DEC 1942.

To The Glory of God

CHANGI LYCH GATE

This is the original Lych Gate from Changi Jail, Singapore, designed by Captain C.D. Pickersgill and built in 1942 by men from the 18th Division who were prisoners of war.

The gate was first erected at the entrance to the camp cemetery to mark the graves of those who had died and to give their funerals some dignity. In 1952, the graves were moved to Kranji War Memorial Cemetery and the Lych Gate to the British Garrison Church in Singapore. When British troops withdrew completely from Singapore in 1971, the Lych Gate was dismantled and brought back to England where it was erected at the Queen's Division Depot, Bassingbourn Barracks in Royston, Hertfordshire. In 2003 the refurbished Lych Gate was reconstructed at the Arboretum by the 39th Engineering Regiment and the re-dedication took place on 8 February 2004.

THE FAR EAST PRISONERS OF WAR MEMORIAL BUILDING

On 16 December 1994, an article in a local newspaper made an incredible impact on one woman who read it, so much so that three years later it brought about the beginning of COFEPOW – The Children (& Families) of the Far East Prisoners of War.

As Carol Cooper from Norfolk started to read the newspaper article, she realised with a tremendous shock that the soldier concerned was her father, a father who was sent to war when she was two years old.

The members of COFEPOW are the children and families of many thousands of men who died on the Thai/Burma railway, the Sumatra railway, the Sandakan Death Marches, in copper mines in Formosa, steel factories in Japan, building roads in Burma and air strips on Ambon, Haruka, Java, Rabaul, New Guinea and the Solomons. Thousands died on the 'Hellships', battened down in holds of unmarked ships and torpedoed by Allied submarines. In addition, thousands were captured and died when Hong Kong fell to the Japanese in December 1941.

The incarceration was not restricted to service personnel – many of the Far East prisoners were civilian internees.

Thousands survived to return after the war and for them the suffering continued for years afterwards. Many of the Association's members bear testament to their fathers' constant nightmares and recurring illnesses.

COFEPOW established the Far East Prisoners of War Memorial Building, not only to remember those who died, but also to encompass the whole story of events during this unprecedented chapter in British history. The memorial roll contains the name and rank of all British Servicemen taken prisoner during the South East Asia conflict and embraces the story of their treatment and the thousands who died as a result.

The Java Memorial consists of two specially commissioned painted windows, replicas of the two made by Lt Cdr Upton, RNVR, for the tiny St George's church, built by the Prisoners of War (POWs) at Tandjong Priok.
The original windows were saved after the war and are now on permanent display at the Anglican Church of All Saints in Jakarta. The replicas form a memorial to not only all those held at Tandjong Priok but also all who were taken prisoner by the Japanese and held captive in Java.

The Far East Prisoners of War Memorial Building was officially opened on 15 August 2005, the 60th anniversary of the end of World War II in the Far East.

Photo by Barry Turner

THE SUMATRA RAILWAY

The Sumatra Railway was constructed in extreme conditions on and around the Equator by 5,000 Allied prisoners of war (POW) and 30,000 local people. The railway was finished on 15 August 1945 (now known as VJ Day), so it was never used except to transport the prisoners on their journey home, and within a very short time it had disappeared back into the bamboo. The late Jack Plant, a veteran who worked on the railway, was inspired to construct the memorial by a sketch drawn by fellow POW Owen Greenwood, showing a stretch of the Railway under construction. The memorial remembers those who died, and asks for peace and reconciliation.

The memorial itself is made from material sourced in the UK, including replicas of the telegraph wires that were placed along the railway, and the correct type of (British) rail tracks. Along the track are tools used in the original construction. The wording and illustrations on the brick memorial plinth describe the conditions and dangers that were endured by the prisoners. On both sides of the railway, European and Japanese maple, rowan and cherry trees have been planted.

JUDY – WHO WAS SHE?

'Judy' was a pure bred English Pointer, a Royal Navy mascot who got herself marooned off Sumatra (Dutch East Indies) during 1942.

A young Airman named Frank Williams took to her and vice versa. He became a Japanese POW but she never left him and stayed with him the whole time. Frank used to feed her, giving up a portion of his small ration of rice. Occasionally she would slip out of camp and get hold of food for herself. It was on one such occasion that she got herself pregnant and duly produced the puppies. The Japanese Camp Commander had one for himself.

She survived gunshot wounds, alligator bites, attacks from wild dogs and even from a tiger. She returned with Frank in August 1945 upon his release. Back in the UK, she was awarded the Dickin Medal (the animals' VC for bravery).

Photo by Barry Turner

229

THE FAR EAST PRISONERS OF WAR GROVE

The Far East Prisoners of War (FEPOW) Grove is approached through the Changi Lych Gate, originally in the POW Cemetery in Singapore. On its right is the memorial of the National Federation of FEPOW Clubs and Associations who were amongst the first to make a donation to the Arboretum. On its left is a map of the Japanese Empire six months after the outbreak of war in the Far East.

Half of the approximately 50,000 British Service men captured by the Japanese in World War II were forced to work on the Burma/Thai Railway. Other FEPOWs worked building airfields and roads, and many were transported to Japan to work in mines, shipbuilding yards and other heavy industries and approximately 800 British POWs were amongst those who built a railway in Sumatra.

Most of the trees in the Grove are dedicated to individual FEPOWs from all three services and internees. Other trees relate to groups of FEPOWs and four of these are worthy of special mention:

- The estimated 1,000 UK FEPOWs who died in North Borneo, principally on the Death Marches.

- The estimated 600 UK FEPOWs transported from Singapore who died in or near the Solomon Islands.

- All FEPOWs lost at sea while being transported.

- The civilian and military women and children who perished.

BURMA RAILWAY

The memorial has been constructed from 30 metres of the original rails and sleepers used on the Burma Railway, which were returned to the Arboretum from Thailand in HMS Northumberland in 2002.

The memorial is a permanent tribute to those who were forced to construct the infamous 'Railway of Death' and the benches and trees around the railway track have relevant dedications. The memorial was dedicated on 15 August 2002.

Photo by Barry Turner

WOMEN'S AUXILIARY SERVICE – THE CHINTHE WOMEN

The Women's Auxiliary Service (Burma), WAS(B), ran canteens for the Fourteenth Army between 1942 and 1946. They operated close to the frontline, supplying tea, cake and sundries to troops. The Army came to regard them as essential for keeping up troop morale.

They were kept busy manning the static canteen 24 hours a day and mobile canteens used for visiting the troops. As well as supplying food they also sold cigarettes, tobacco, razor blades and other shop items.

They got a reputation for being of value for giving morale and getting stores. It was important that the men could buy their own cigarettes. Chief Commandant Nin Taylor held it together. She was a strong woman and did not take no for an answer. She wanted to go as far forward as possible, but the Divisional Generals were not very happy about having them there.

WOMEN'S AUXILIARY SERVICE (BURMA) 1942 - 1946 In memory of those whose canteens served on the front line in BURMA (X1V Army) also India, Java, Sumatra,

Photo by Phil Nixon

THE HONG KONG VOLUNTEER DEFENCE CORPS

The HKVDC was mobilised in early December 1941. Following the Japanese invasion on the 8th December, the Corps fought in defence of Hong Kong. Overwhelmed, the fighting ceased on Christmas Day. Over 200 volunteers were killed in the battle and a further 70 died as prisoners of war.

A number of volunteers escaped from the territory and made their way to India where they formed a Hong Kong Volunteer Company. Some of them subsequently fought in Burma with the Chindits.

Lt. Colonel R. J. L. Penfold of the Royal Artillery, writing in 1946, said this, "To fight where he dwells is probably the most distasteful task a soldier faces." It was in the few days of the battle, fighting among the ruins of their homes, that the HKDVC truly confirmed the right to its motto "Nulli Secundus" or second to none.

Photo by By Phil Nixon

ROYAL NORFOLK REGIMENT, SUFFOLK REGIMENT AND CAMBRIDGESHIRE REGIMENT MEMORIAL

The Royal Norfolk Regiment, originally known as Colonel Cornwall's Regiment of Foot, was the second of eight infantry regiments raised by James II to suppress the Monmouth rebellion in 1685. In 1799, HM King George III officially conferred the honour of wearing the figure 'Britannia' as the badge of the Regiment. The 9th was re-titled The Norfolk Regiment and "Rule Britannia" was adopted as the Regimental march in 1881. In June 1935, HM King George V bestowed the honour of the prefix 'Royal' in the title of the Regiment. Five members of the Regiment were awarded the Victoria Cross during World War II, a greater number than any other regiment in the British Army.

The Suffolk Regiment was formed in 1685, as The Duke of Norfolk's (12th) Regiment of Foot. The links with the county of Suffolk were recognised in 1783 when the Regiment was restyled the 12th (East Suffolk) Regiment.

The Regiment reformed in 1947 as 629 (The Cambridgeshire Regiment) Light Anti-Aircraft Regiment RA TA, retaining its cap badge and colours. In 1956, the Regiment reverted to infantry as the 1st Battalion the Cambridgeshire Regiment, but was amalgamated with 4 Suffolk in 1961 to become 1st Battalion Suffolk and Cambridgeshire Regiment, and was disbanded in 1967.

Photo by David Faul

BURMA STAR

The Burma Star Association was founded in 1951 for World War II veterans holding the Burma Campaign Star or the Pacific Star with Burma Clasp. The Association's broad aims are to promote the comradeship experienced during those hard times of war and to provide assistance in cases of hardship and distress to veterans, widows and dependants. Some 60 years later, the Association still has around 6,000 members worldwide with 100 branches operating in the UK and nine overseas.

The war in the Far East started in December 1941, with the bombing of Pearl Harbour. From early 1942, the Japanese army advanced relentlessly into Burma heading for India. The next three years saw ferocious fighting in the most inhospitable terrain and dense jungle, with extremes of weather further exacerbated by malaria and other tropical diseases.

The Fourteenth Army, known to many as 'the Forgotten Army', numbered over one million men under arms, the largest Commonwealth army ever assembled. The Japanese surrendered on 15 August 1945, now known as VJ Day.

The Battle of Kohima was one of the bloodiest battles fought in Burma, with the British and Japanese armies fighting in close proximity, separated only by the British Administrator's tennis court.

The memorial here is a smaller replica of the one which stands in the Commonwealth War Cemetery in Kohima and bears the words of the famous Kohima Epitaph which is so poignant to all of those veterans who came home.

Photo by Barry Turner

THE CHINDIT MEMORIAL

After the 1942 campaign, 77 Brigade was reformed as an airborne force consisting of 1st South Staffords, 1st Kings, 1st Lancashire Fusiliers and 3/6 Ghurkhas, becoming part of 3rd Division.

Shortly after landing in Burma, the Brigade was engaged with and successfully defeated a strong Japanese force at Mawlu on the railway north of Mandalay. This first engagement became known as the battle of Pagoda Hill, the fighting was principally hand to hand and there were heavy casualties on both sides. This was where Lieutenant George Cairns, of the Staffords, was posthumously awarded the Victoria Cross.

77 Brigade continued to hold Mawlu for two months, thus denying supplies by rail to Japanese forces in the Arakan and North Burma, which seriously impaired their campaigns in those areas.

Tragically, the Chindit Force Commander, Major General Orde Wingate, was killed. So was lost an outstanding leader of whom Winston Churchill said "… he might well have become a man of destiny".

Photo by By Phil Nixon

Photo by Barry Turner

THE ROTARY RIDGE

The hedge of golden Castlewellan cypress that acts as a windbreak and backdrop to the Arboretum, was first sponsored by local clubs in Rotary District 1060 as a tribute to the Rotary Clubs in Great Britain and Ireland and Rotary International, whose motto is "Service above Self".

Trees are also dedicated to individual clubs and Rotarians. Local Rotary Clubs have enthusiastically supported the Arboretum from the early years with individual Rotarians volunteering their skills, business contacts and expertise in many fields.

BRITISH KOREAN VETERANS ASSOCIATION

In 1950, 22 member nations of the United Nations (UN) joined South Korean forces to repel the North Korean aggression and stop the spread of Communism. During the three years of the conflict, some four million people died. Over 100,000 British Service personnel served during the war, of whom over 2,000 were killed or taken prisoner. Among many decorations awarded were four Victoria Crosses and two George Crosses.

In 1952, the Commonwealth units from Australia, Canada, India, New Zealand and South Africa combined to form the 1st Commonwealth Division.

The memorial garden, originally laid out and maintained by members of the British Korean Veterans Association (BKVA), is designed to create a living memorial to all British Service Personnel who served and gave their lives. It is an arboretum within an arboretum, planted with more than 100 trees of some 23 different species, mostly of Korean or Asian origin.

Photo by By Phil Nixon

Photo by Barry Turner

17TH DOGRA REGIMENT

The Dogra Regiment was raised in 1887 from the foothills of the Himalayas and earned laurels for valour in both World Wars, including Nunshigam, Imphal and Kota Bharu in the World War II Burma campaign. In the pre-independence era, before 1947, the regiment earned three Victoria Crosses (VC) and 44 Military Crosses in addition to 312 other awards.

One of the VCs was awarded to Lance Corporal Naik Lala while serving in Mesopotamia in 1916. He tended and rescued two wounded officers while under heavy shell fire, one of them being Captain Nicholson (later Major General F L Nicholson, CB DSO MC and Colonel of the 1st Battalion from 1934 until 1948), whose name appears on the Regiment's commemorative plaque.

Photo by By Phil Nixon

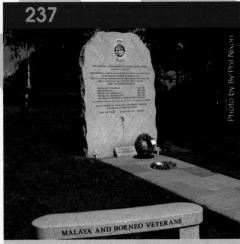

Photo by By Phil Nixon

MALAYA AND BORNEO VETERANS

BRIGADE OF GURKHAS

Gurkhas have served the British Crown for almost 200 years. It is a rich heritage marked by excellence and sacrifice. The history of the Brigade from its inception in 1815 during the early wars between the Honorable East India Company and city-state of Gorkha, through the early Afghan wars, the two World Wars, the almost continuous post-war conflicts to modern day Afghanistan are forged from the deep feeling of mutual respect and admiration developed between the British and their Gurkha adversaries.

Following the Nepal Wars, and under the terms of the Sugauli Peace Treaty in 1816, Gurkhas were permitted to volunteer for service in the East India Company's Army. From these volunteers were formed the first regiments of the Gurkha Brigade, and from this time stems Britain's friendship with Nepal, a country which has proved a staunch ally ever since and has become our 'oldest ally' in Asia. Never has the trust that was then placed in the Gurkha soldier ever been in doubt.

Since 1997, the Brigade of Gurkhas has been operationally and battle proven in Bosnia, Kosovo, East Timor, Sierra Leone, Macedonia and Iraq. With 11 years of continuous Gurkha deployments in Afghanistan, the human cost and sacrifice in Afghanistan has been high. 54 officers and soldiers of the Brigade have been wounded in action and 15 have made the ultimate sacrifice.

MALAYA AND BORNEO VETERANS MEMORIAL

This memorial is dedicated to the many thousands of men who fought in Malaysia, Borneo, Singapore and Brunei. The 6' 10" by 4' 11" granite stone is expected to last 2000 years, providing a lasting memorial to the estimated 30,000 men who fought in World War II, the Malayan Emergency, The Confrontation and further conflicts in south east Asia. It is intended as a place of quiet reflection for thousands of men and their families, remembering those who made the ultimate sacrifice and those who have departed subsequent to the end of hostilities.

ROYAL MALAYSIA POLICE

The memorial is dedicated to all ranks of the former Malayan, Singaporean and Bornean Police Forces, subsequently united in the Royal Malaysia Police. All these forces took part in World War II and subsequent counter-insurgency campaigns fighting alongside Commonwealth military forces between 1948 and 1989.

In the 'Malayan Emergency', the Royal Malaysia Police suffered 1,300 fatalities.

Dedicated to all ranks of the former Malayan Singapore and Bornean Police forces Subsequently united in the Royal Malaysia Police Especially remembering those who gave their lives in the Second World War and later campaigns 1948-1989

Photo by By Phil Nixon

MALAYAN VOLUNTEER FORCE

The Malayan Volunteers Group, mostly children of volunteers with some veterans, was formed in 2005 to commemorate and raise awareness of the Malayan volunteers in the Malayan Campaign and captivity 1941 – 1945.

Some 18,000 volunteers of different races and creeds served in the Malayan Volunteer Forces, Medical Auxiliary Service and Observer Corps, receiving 100 Campaign Awards. In captivity, they contributed practical and medical skills, knowledge of local languages and secret radios, saving lives and giving hope of victory. Others taught in 'Changi University'.

SULTAN OF OMAN'S ARMED FORCES MEMORIAL

Photo by Phil Nixon

The truncated pyramid-shaped plinth with its plaque, maps and badge, together with four trees of the variety Cypressus sempervirens, form a memorial in recognition of all who served in or supported the Armed Forces of the Sultanate of Oman.

Since their formal establishment in the early 1950s, with British assistance, these forces have twice overcome insurgencies which have threatened the integrity or social structure of the state, and more recently have contributed contingents or facilities to coalitions formed to protect the Persian Gulf states.

They still enjoy a close relationship with the British Military.

BALUCH REGIMENT

The Regiment was raised in 1820 as a Regiment of Indian Native Infantry and renamed successively The Baluchistan Regiment Bombay Infantry (1895), The Baluchistan Infantry (1902) and The 10th Baluch Regiment (1922).

They served loyally and in amity under British and Indian officers and fought in campaigns in Abyssinia in 1868, in China in 1900 and in Europe during World War I 1914 – 15. Officers who were privileged to lead and serve in the regiment sponsored the grove.

THE GREEN ZONE

Access: Some access from the hard paved Millennium Avenue but most is from 'The Beat' which is a mown grass avenue.

Terrain: Firm surface and mown grassland.

Starting point: From Visitor Centre, turn right into Millennium Avenue and begin walk from the large gate leading to the car park entrance.

No	Memorial	Pg
©️	ARMED FORCES MEMORIAL	9
301	NORMANDY VETERANS	67
302	KING'S AFRICAN RIFLES	67
303	THE ROYAL ENGINEERS	68
304	THE FREEMASONS	68
305	THE BEAT (POLICE MEMORIAL AVENUE)	69
305	SPECIAL CONSTABULARY	70
306	POLICE MEMORIAL GARDEN	70
307	THE POLAR BEAR MEMORIAL	71
308	BROTHERHOOD OF GREEK VETERANS CHAPEL	72
309	CAVALRY GROVE (CRESCENT)	73
310	THE PHANTOM MEMORIAL	73
311	THE ARMY PARADE	75
311c	YORKSHIRE REGIMENT	75

No	Memorial	Pg
311a	THE ROYAL GREEN JACKETS	75
311b	10TH ROYAL HUSSARS	76
311b	11TH ROYAL HUSSARS (THE CHERRY PICKERS)	76
312	WAR WIDOWS' WOOD AND MEMORIAL	76
313	MEDITERRANEAN CAMPAIGNS OF WORLD WAR II	77
313	THE ROYAL HAMPSHIRE REGIMENT	78
313	THE WAR WIDOWS' ROSE GARDEN	79
313	GARDEN OF THE INNOCENTS	79
313a	THE ARMY WOOD	80
313b	ARMY AIR CORPS	80
314	ROYAL LOGISTIC CORPS	81
315	KENYA POLICE	82

No	Memorial	Pg
316	ROYAL MILITARY POLICE ASSOCIATION	82
317	SOROPTIMIST INTERNATIONAL	83
318	BRITISH GERMAN FRIENDSHIP GARDEN	83
319	ANGLO-JAPANESE PEACE GARDEN	84
320	CELEBRATION OF LIFE GROVE	84
321	IRAQ / AFGHANISTAN WILLOWS	84
321a	BASRA MEMORIAL WALL	85
322	THE NAVY WOOD	85
323	THE BLUES AND ROYALS	86
324	ROYAL TANK REGIMENT	86
325	MERCIAN WOOD	86
325a	ROYAL CORPS OF SIGNALS	87
326	IRISH INFANTRY GROVE	87
327	COMMANDER DAVID CHILDS' TREES	87
327	THE GOLDEN GROVE	88
327	THE QUEEN ALEXANDRA'S ROYAL ARMY NURSING CORPS	88
327a	POLISH FORCES WAR MEMORIAL (E)	89
328	ROYAL ARMY MEDICAL CORPS	91
328	ROYAL ARMY DENTAL CORPS	92
329	SHOT AT DAWN (D)	93
330	LICHFIELD WOOD	95
330	ROYAL GLOUCESTERSHIRE, BERKSHIRE AND WILTSHIRE REGIMENT	96
330a	THE SHOWMEN'S GUILD OF GREAT BRITAIN	97
331	KINGFISHER WOOD	98
331	GCHQ MEMORIAL	98
331	THE INTELLIGENCE CORPS	98
331	BIRMINGHAM CHILDREN'S HOSPITAL	99
331a	ARMY APPRENTICE NATIONAL MEMORIAL	99
332	HOUSEHOLD DIVISION	100
332	LIGHT INFANTRY MEMORIAL	101
332	THE DURHAM LIGHT INFANTRY	102
332	THE MALL	102
332	1ST THE QUEEN'S DRAGOON GUARDS	102
332	THE PARACHUTE REGIMENT AND AIRBORNE FORCES	103
332	ROYAL ELECTRICAL AND MECHANICAL ENGINEERS (REME)	104
333	ROYAL AIR FORCE WOOD	104
334	ROYAL AIR FORCE CRANWELL APPRENTICES	105

No	Memorial	Pg
335	ROYAL AIR FORCE BOY ENTRANTS	105
336	COASTAL COMMAND	105
336	RAF LOCKING	106
336	THE RAIL INDUSTRY	106
336	GIRLS VENTURE CORPS	107
336	RAF ADMINISTRATIVE APPRENTICES	107
336	THE CHELTENHAM COLLEGE MEMORIAL	107
337	WOMEN'S SECTION, THE ROYAL BRITISH LEGION	107
337	ROYAL NATIONAL LIFEBOAT INSTITUTION	108
337a	SHACKLETON ASSOCIATION MEMORIAL	109
338	THE 41 CLUB	110
339	ANCIENT BURIAL MOUND	111
340	THE ROYAL OBSERVER CORPS	111
340	II (ARMY COOPERATION) SQUADRON	112
340	RAF BENEVOLENT FUND	112
340a	ROYAL AIR FORCES ASSOCIATION REMEMBRANCE GARDEN	113
341	ROYAL & SUN ALLIANCE MEMORIALS	115
341a	NO 30 SQUADRON ASSOCIATION	115
342	ROYAL AIR FORCE SERVICING COMMANDO AND TACTICAL SUPPLY WING ASSOCIATION	116
343	ROYAL AUXILIARY AIR FORCE	116
343a	AIRCREW ASSOCIATION MEMORIAL	117
344	ROYAL CANADIAN AIR FORCE	117
344	ROYAL AIR FORCE WING	118
344a	THE ROYAL AIR FORCE POLICE	118
345	WOMEN'S AUXILIARY AIR FORCE (WAAF)	119
346	AIR FORMATION AND AIR SUPPORT SIGNALS	119
346a	90 SIGNALS UNIT	120
347	ROYAL AUSTRALIAN AIR FORCE	120
348	ADJUTANT GENERAL'S CORPS COMMEMORATIVE GARDEN	120
349	STAFFORDSHIRE REGIMENT	121
350	ASSOCIATION OF JEWISH EX-SERVICEMEN AND WOMEN	121
350a	THE SHRIEVALTY AVENUE	122
351	GALLIPOLI	122
352	MERCIAN VOLUNTEERS	123
353	HOME SERVICE FORCE	123
354	TOC H	124

"I'M GLAD IT WAS RECOGNISED AT LONG LAST – IT'S A LONG TIME AFTER THE WAR."

Veteran Feliks Keidrowski commented on the Polish Armed Forces Memorial and its recognition of Poland's contribution to the Allied war effort.

Photo by Barry Turner

NORMANDY VETERANS

The Normandy Veterans' memorial was dedicated on 9 August 1999 and became a focus of the 60th Anniversary Commemorations of the 6 June 1944 'D' Day Allied Assault, when there was a live video link with the ceremonies attended by HM The Queen in France.

The avenue of poplar trees, memorial plinth and five stones named for each of the Normandy beaches Utah, Omaha, Gold, Juno and Sword are dedicated to all the men and women who took part in the Normandy Campaign of 1944.

KING'S AFRICAN RIFLES

The King's African Rifles (KAR) started its illustrious career in 1902, battalions being found from Nyasaland, Kenya, Uganda, Tanganyika and later incorporating Northern Rhodesia. Its first major confrontation was in the Tanganyika Campaign fighting the Germans under General Paul von Lettow-Vorbeck. From 1940 – 1942 battalions were engaged in Eritrea, Abyssinia and Somaliland against the Italians and later in Madagascar. Many battalions moved into Burma from 1944 to the end of fighting there, and after the war were deployed in combating insurgency in Malaya and Kenya.

The African soldiers came from a wide variety of tribes and were renowned for their fortitude, good humour and strong sense of discipline. Those lucky enough to have served with them had the privilege of their devoted tenacity and friendship.

The KAR Association has now assumed the duty in providing for the urgent welfare of many old men and widows throughout East Africa.

Photo by Barry Turner

THE ROYAL ENGINEERS

The memorial was dedicated in the presence of The Chief Royal Engineer, General Sir Kevin O'Donoghue KCB CBE, during a ceremony on 1 May 2007 and commemorates all Royal Engineers ('Sappers') who have fallen in the past and will do so in the future.

The central features of the monument are four granite rocks each weighing approximately 10 tonnes which were presented to the Corps of Royal Engineers by the people of the Falkland Islands. These four large random blocks of granite present a challenge, which is both physical and visual, in bringing them together to form an appropriate and satisfying Memorial. Their weight and mass create an interesting engineering problem which is visually expressed to illustrate the work of the Corps of Royal Engineers. The four stones are placed in a circle and each is raised 150mm above its concrete foundation on several stainless steel dowels, making the huge blocks appear to float above the grass, suggesting a visual metaphor of the ability of the Sapper to intervene in, and control, the physical and geographical environment.

THE FREEMASONS

The light and dark grey paving reflects the joys and sorrows of our chequered existence. In addition, there are two large stones, one of rough ashlar representing man in his prime and the other polished smooth to represent man in his later years having benefited from education and learning.

Since the cutting of 'the first sod' on 25 June 2002, the garden is being developed gradually and is designed to include Masonic symbolism that can be readily understood by everyone. The memorial will take decades to reach its true beauty and maturity, but from its earliest stages of construction is a fitting and resilient memorial to past sacrifices and mankind's hopes for the future.

Photo by Barry Turner

Photo by OceanBarefoot

305

THE BEAT (POLICE MEMORIAL AVENUE)

The Beat (Police Memorial Avenue) is planted with a tree for every police force in the UK, their force crest is displayed on a plaque beside each tree. Between the force trees are individual dedications to those who have died on duty, together with trees for police representative associations. Chestnut trees were chosen because the first policemen 'peelers' or 'bobbies' carried truncheons made from this wood. The Beat was sponsored by Police Mutual and was opened in September 1997 by the then Home Secretary The Rt. Hon Jack Straw MP.

Each year, Care of Police Survivors (COPS), a charity that provides support to the families of officers killed on duty, hold a service of Remembrance on 'The Beat'.

SPECIAL CONSTABULARY

This monument is in recognition of the dedication to duty by members of the Special Constabulary protecting and serving their communities and to commemorate those Specials who have died in service to their country. The Special Constabulary is the part time volunteer section of the Police force in the United Kingdom.

They were redefined during World War I, where they were instructed to safeguard water supplies from German infiltrators. During World War II, besides their normal duties, they were trained to deal with a range of eventualities such as first aid in case of injury, initial co-ordination of the security of aircraft crash sites, clearing people from the vicinity of unexploded bombs, handling of unignited incendiary bombs and checking compliance with lighting regulations. The memorial was kindly donated by the people of the communities of the West Midlands region.

Photo by David Faul

POLICE MEMORIAL GARDEN

The Police Credit Union sponsors and maintains the memorial garden, designed to be a place of peace and contemplation with its individually dedicated trees, benches and memorial plaques.

At the entrance to the garden is a memorial chestnut tree grown from a conker collected from the grounds of Drayton Manor Park, the former home of Robert Peel, the founder of the modern police force.

Photo by Barry Turner

Photo by OceanBarefoot

THE POLAR BEAR MEMORIAL

The Polar Bear Association Memorial was the first monument and sculpture to be placed in the Arboretum. It is a tribute to the 49th Infantry West Riding Division and was dedicated on 7 June 1998. Inheriting the fine reputation forged by its predecessor in World War I, World War II found the 49th Infantry stationed in Iceland and, because they were snowed in 20 feet of snow for most of the campaign, their commanding officer called the men 'his Polar Bears'. The Polar Bear on a block of ice was soon adopted as their mascot and shoulder flash.

Made from yellow hardwood, the bear is 9ft long and 5ft high and weighs 2.5 tonnes; it was created by the Essex Woodcarvers and took a year to carve. Inside the bear is a time capsule containing the names of all the members of the 49th Division who did not come home, together with relevant letters and documents.

In the panels set into the brick base of the monument are carvings of the badges of the Regiments of the 49th Infantry with two panels containing the poems written by schoolgirl Jodie Johnson when she was only nine and 11 years of age.

BROTHERHOOD OF GREEK VETERANS CHAPEL

The impressive Greek stone and marble altar in this chapel symbolises the strength of this Brotherhood that was established in April 1991 commemorating the 50th Anniversary of the surrender of The Allied Forces at Kalamata, The Peloponnese and Southern Greece. 10,000 men were captured and became POWs, enduring massive hardship and terrifying trials until Liberation. The horrors of war and incarceration created a band of spirited and brave young men whose camaraderie and resilience survives even to this day.

EUROPE 1943 – SECOND ATTEMPTED ESCAPE FROM POW CAMP – FRANK GILL

"Let me tell you, that escaping was no picnic! It indeed was a nerve-wracking, heart-stopping event. The tension was terrible; every movement we heard was treated with suspicion. Every rustle of leaves brought uneasiness. Even your mates' voices, suddenly asking a hushed question, caused the blood to flow faster.

Why then, you may ask, bother to break out at all? Well, adventure and the fact that one's youth was wasting away and one needed to do something to prove that life still held some sort of challenge… Eventually, after a couple of hours, we emerged from the darkened wood. It was a moonlit night and as such the night had helped our exploits in crossing the exposed road, so it also became our downfall!"

Photo by Phil Nixon

CAVALRY GROVE (CRESCENT)

This grove consists of a colourful mix of ornamental trees and memorials dedicated to the Cavalry Regiments of the British Army. These include 9/12 Lancers, The 17/21 Lancers, The Queen's Royal Hussars, The Royal Dragoon Guards and The Queen's Royal Lancers.

Photo by Barry Turner

THE PHANTOM MEMORIAL

The Phantoms were a wireless communication unit for the Special Air Service (SAS). The Memorial particularly remembers events of 1944 when F Squadron was in France to provide communications for Operation Loyton.

The path is laid out in a P design to denote the word Phantom; 140 plants represent the 140 men and boys who did not return from concentration camps.

The coral granite memorial stone was cut from a much larger stone at Senone, a few miles from Moussey, and represents the resolve of the villagers and resistance forces that protected the soldiers on the operation. The Cross of Lorraine was later added to the memorial to represent the Anglo / Norman link.

The late Len Owens, who served in the unit and sponsored the memorial, has written:

Three men of Phantom Signals were killed: two in combat and one man was betrayed, captured, tortured and then killed. 31 men of 2 SAS were killed, the majority killed after capture.

But these losses were small compared with those suffered by the citizens of Moussey and the surrounding area. 220 men and boys were taken to Gestapo HQ and anyone giving information about the SAS was to be allowed to go free. Nobody moved and consequently all were sent to concentration camps named Dachau and Matthausen. Of these, 140 did not return. The Mayor of Moussey, Monsieur Jacques Defrance, asked if these 140 could be named on the Phantom Memorial. This was done along with the names of the 31 SAS men who were killed, again mostly after capture. The names of the four British Service women are also given. They were first killed by lethal injection but one recovered and was pushed into the ovens while alive.

PHANTOM GARDEN

Photo by Barry Turner

311

THE ARMY PARADE

The Army Parade is laid out in a formal pattern based on the fighting square with dedicated trees, plaques and plinths representing most of the infantry regiments of the British Army.

311c

YORKSHIRE REGIMENT

The Yorkshire Regiment was formed from three former regiments: The Green Howards, The Prince of Wales' Own Regiment of Yorkshire and the Duke of Wellington's Regiment.

311a

THE ROYAL GREEN JACKETS

On 11 May 2008, over 1,100 former Royal Green Jackets (RGJ) gathered with pride to remember all those who served in the RGJ for the forty years of the Regiment's existence (1966 – 2007) and to dedicate this memorial to them.

The memorial is of black polished Indian granite and weighs just over two tonnes. It is flanked by Remembrance Trees of the three forming regiments of the RGJ (Oxfordshire, Buckinghamshire Light Infantry, Kings Royal Rifle Corps and Rifle Brigade). A small plaque is placed by the memorial commemorating the dedication event and the unveiling by Field Marshal The Lord Bramall of Bushfield.

The adjacent Armed Forces Memorial has 72 names of RGJ Riflemen and 61 names of the forming regiments of the Royal Green Jackets who were killed on duty or as a result of terrorist action since World War II.

Photo by David Faul

SWIFT and BOLD
THIS MEMORIAL IS DEDICATED TO
THE OFFICERS AND RIFLEMEN OF
THE ROYAL GREEN JACKETS
1st JANUARY 1966 – 31st JANUARY 2007

10TH ROYAL HUSSARS

At the time of the First Jacobite Rebellion in 1715, the 10th Regiment of Dragoons was raised in Herefordshire by Brigadier Humphrey Gore. The regiment campaigned in the Peninsula War and fought at Waterloo. The 10th were in the Crimea and were awarded two VCs in the South African War.

In 1784, HM King George III appointed his son, then Prince of Wales, as Colonel of the Regiment which has since borne the title of 'Prince of Wales' Own' with the coronet and feathers, together with the Rising Sun and Red Dragon (an ancient badge of Wales) and the motto "Ich Dien" ("I serve"). In 1806, the Prince of Wales obtained permission to clothe and equip the regiment as Hussars and it thus became the First Hussar Regiment in the British Army. The 10th Royal Hussars has taken part in most of the campaigns of the British Army from the Seven Years War in 1758 to the War of 1939 – 1945 and has seen service in most parts of the world. On 25 October 1969, the 10th Royal Hussars amalgamated with the 11th Hussars to form the Royal Hussars.

Photo by Barry Turner

11TH ROYAL HUSSARS
(THE CHERRY PICKERS)

The Regiment was formed in 1715. Notable personalities include Lord Cardigan, who led the Regiment in the Charge of the Light Brigade and Prince Albert (husband of Queen Victoria) from whom the Regiment got its famous cherry coloured trousers. The nickname Cherrypickers came after an action in a cherry orchard.

In World War II, the Regiment led the Desert Rats, the 7th Armoured Division, and were the first British troops into Berlin. The 77 battle honours shown on the memorial tell the full story. The Regiment was amalgamated with the 10th Royal Hussars in 1969.

312

Photo by Barry Turner

WAR WIDOWS' WOOD AND MEMORIAL

This planting is a mixture of individually dedicated native trees sponsored by war widows in memory of their husbands who never returned from conflict.

MEDITERRANEAN CAMPAIGNS OF WORLD WAR II

The Mediterranean Garden is laid out geographically with, at the far side, the outline of the North African coast. Here, trees native to that region have been planted to commemorate those who served with the 1st and 8th Armies. There is also a stone memorial to the famous Rats of Tobruk who endured one of the longest sieges in British and Commonwealth military history. Another stone plinth recalls those who served in Palestine before Israel gained independence. The near side the garden, in the shape of Sicily and Italy, has been planted with Black Pine, each tree linked to one of the major battles of the Italian Campaign. The Siege of Malta 1940 – 1943 is commemorated by a brick built, shrub-planted Cross of St John. The Italy Star Association 1943 – 1945 was founded in 1987 by late brothers Eric and Maurice Cheadle (veterans of North Africa and Italy), and remains active, keeping alive that special bond of comradeship from the Italian campaigns. The outline of Sicily and mainland Italy has a simple stone memorial overlooking the site which was dedicated to the Association in 2001.

Memorials and trees in this garden, relevant to the Mediterranean Campaigns are below:

- The Palestine Veterans' Association
- The Palestine Police Old Comrades' Association
- 8th Army and Tobruk
- 1st Army
- George Cross Island Association (Malta)
- Italy Star Association 1943 – 1945
- The Monte Cassino Memorial
- Cyprus Veterans

Dedicated to the memory of the ALLIED FORCES who fought for the capture of MONTE CASSINO during the Italian campaign January to May 1944

ROYAL HAMPSHIRE REGIMENT

The Royal Hampshire Regiment served this country from 1702 to 1992 and played its part in the major campaigns which saw the gaining and relinquishing of the largest Empire the world has ever seen.

After the 67th had served in India from 1805 – 1826, it was decreed that the Colours and other appointments were to bear the figure of the Royal Tiger with the word 'India'. The plinth below tells the story of the Regiment both graphically and in words. Sara Ingleby-Mackenzie was the sculptor and the stonework was by Nick Johnson.

Photo by Phil Nixon

Photo by Phil Nixon

Photo by OceanBarefoot

THE WAR WIDOWS' ROSE GARDEN

The Rose Garden has been planted as a tribute to the Nation's war widows who often endure great hardship, as well as emotional stress, through the loss of their husbands.

The Rose Garden design has four sections and takes visitors along the terrible journey of bereavement through the colours of the roses. The emotional trip starts with the reds of anger, into the purples of despair, then passes through the gentler colours of quiet acceptance and finally into the yellows of happy memories.

313

Photo by Phil Nixon

GARDEN OF THE INNOCENTS

The Garden of the Innocents is a memorial to all child victims of war and terrorism.

The theme of the Garden is portrayed in green and white, symbolising innocence, with raised beds in the shape of jigsaw pieces which do not fit together, symbolising the confusion and bewilderment children suffer through war and violence.

The central tree is an elder planted in memory of Anne Frank. The blossoms of the tree are cut each year on 12 June, the anniversary of Anne's birthday, so the tree never bears fruit, just as Anne herself was prevented from reaching maturity.

THE ARMY WOOD

The Army Wood consists of mixed native trees individually sponsored and dedicated to those who have served in the British Armed Forces. In the wood is a memorial to the Army Air Corps.

Photo by Phil Nixon

ARMY AIR CORPS

The modern Army Air Corps was formed at Middle Wallop on 1 September 1957. The decision to bring together the various elements of Army Aviation under the Army Air Corps in 1957 was, in part, recognition of its value as an integral element of the land battle but was also a platform to the future. The result was the establishment of a Corps that continued to deliver those familiar services of Army Aviation whilst developing and experimenting with new strategies, equipment and tactics.

The Army Air Corps has come a long way in the last 50 years. It has retained those roles that it inherited in the post war years and they have been developed for the modern world. It has added attack, assault and surveillance roles. The Army Air Corps has been an integral part of operations in all theatres from Aden and Borneo through the Falklands Islands, Northern Ireland and the Balkans to Iraq and Afghanistan. Those operations have not been without loss. Over 150 members of Army Aviation have died in service since 1957.

In commemoration of those
Officers and Soldiers
of
The ARMY POSTAL CORPS
and
The ROYAL ENGINEERS
(POSTAL & COURIER SERVICES)
who served their country in war and operations
and
to remember those who gave their lives

UBIQUE

Photo by Barry Turner

ROYAL LOGISTIC CORPS

The grove, including the memorial plinth and surrounding edible wild plants such as bramble, crab apple, hawthorn and rose, was dedicated on 11 September 2000 as a tribute to The Royal Logistic Corps. Since the formation of the Corps in 1993, it has been their responsibility to sustain British Armed forces wherever they are deployed.

During the periods of tension, wars and peacekeeping operations, members of the Corps have been awarded the George Cross and George Medal, and in the case of the late Warrant Officer 2 (WO2) O'Donnell, a bar to his George Medal.

The RLC serves at sea and in the air, as well as carrying out a number of significant and technical roles on land. The RLC's mission is to "Fight Logistics through" and it delivers whatever the cost.

ROYAL MILITARY POLICE ASSOCIATION

The plinth, flagpole and carved wooden benches of the Royal Military Police Association (RMPA) memorial are dedicated to the men and women of the Military Police who have given their lives in the service of their country. Their motto is Exemplo ducemus, "by example we lead".

The Royal Military Police (RED CAPS) memorial shows the figure of a RMP which was brought to the Arboretum from the old barracks in Chichester and is known as 'FOXY' after Corporal Fox, the model.

A common punishment at the barracks for bad behaviour was to clean the brass plaque on the side of the figure.

KENYA POLICE

The bench, tree and plaques were dedicated on 20 October 2004 to remember all ranks who served in the Kenya Police and Kenya Police Reserve up to the year 1963, when Kenya was granted independence from Britain.

SOROPTIMIST INTERNATIONAL

Soroptimist International, a worldwide organisation for women in management and the professions, is a global voice for women through awareness, advocacy and action.

Soroptimist International is a vibrant, dynamic organisation for today's professional and business women. They are committed to a world where women and girls together achieve their individual and collective potential, realise aspirations and have an equal voice in creating strong, peaceful communities worldwide.

The name Soroptimist derives from the Latin soror, meaning sister, and optima, meaning best. It is best translated as 'best of sisters'.

BRITISH GERMAN FRIENDSHIP GARDEN

This thoughtfully designed peace grove was officially inaugurated by the Duke of Kent in October 2006 to celebrate 60 years of peace and reconciliation between the United Kingdom and Germany.

The garden design has two circles of silver birch and a circle of stones retrieved from the rubble of the Frauenkirche in Dresden which was destroyed by Allied bombing during World War II. Each of the smoke blackened stones displays a plaque bearing the name of a German or British city that suffered heavy damage during the conflict. Sixty thousand British citizens died in German Bombing raids and six hundred thousand German citizens died in raids by the RAF and USAAF. In the centre of the garden is the Dresden Oak, gifted by the Dresden Trust, and nearby stands a Gingko (recalling Goethe's poem) and two trees presented by one-time enemy combatants.

Photo by Phil Nixon

Photo by Phil Nixon

ANGLO-JAPANESE PEACE GARDEN

The Anglo-Japanese Peace Grove was dedicated jointly by the Japanese Ambassador and Mrs. Keiko Holmes on 15 August 2001. Mrs Holmes is the founder president of Agape, the organisation working for reconciliation between Far East Prisoners of War (FEPOWs), their families and the Japanese.

The Reconciliation Stone stands amongst a planting of European and Japanese maples whose brightly coloured leaves will intermingle as they fall in autumn, symbolising friendship between nations that were once bitter enemies. The flowering cherry trees in the adjoining grove were individually sponsored by Japanese businesses and families.

The Hiroshima Memorial Cairn lies on the corner of the garden and is surmounted by a granite stone from the ruins of Hiroshima.

CELEBRATION OF LIFE GROVE

Supported by the Midlands Co-operative Society, the grove is a large semi-circular planting of mixed spring-flowering blossom trees individually dedicated as a celebration of the life of family members and friends who have passed away.

IRAQ / AFGHANISTAN WILLOWS

This planting is a sweeping avenue of weeping willows alongside the Darbyshire Ditch, which are individually sponsored and dedicated to servicemen and women who have lost their lives in Iraq and Afghanistan.

BASRA MEMORIAL WALL

The Basra Memorial Wall is a truly poignant monument to the 178 UK Service personnel and one Ministry of Defence (MOD) civilian who lost their lives on combat operations in Iraq and also lists members of Coalition Forces who were killed whilst under UK command during six years of conflict.

The original memorial was built in Basra in 2006 and stood outside the front of the Headquarters of the Multi-National Division (South East). Following the end of operations, the Basra Memorial Wall was brought back to the UK and rebuilt. The original wall was built and dismantled, and the new wall constructed at the Arboretum by British soldiers from 37th Armoured Engineer Squadron in a personal gesture to commemorate their fallen comrades.

The brass plaques on this memorial are the originals placed on the wall when it was in situ in Basra, Iraq. The plaques are cleaned twice a year; before the anniversary of the end of combat operations in Iraq and before Armistice, but in between they will be allowed to weather naturally. This will allow the details on these original plaques to last for as long as possible for the benefit of future generations.

Photo by Barry Turner

THE NAVY WOOD

The Navy Wood consists of mixed native trees individually sponsored and dedicated to those who have served in the Royal Navy and Merchant Navy.

Photo by Barry Turner

323

THE BLUES AND ROYALS

The curved avenue of blue and gold conifers, the bench and memorial plinth of Derbyshire limestone and polished granite are dedicated to the memory of all ranks of The Royal Horse Guards, The Royal Dragoons and the Blues and Royals who have died whilst in the service of their country at home and overseas from 1945 to the present day.

The Derbyshire limestone memorial stone from Longcliffe Quarries Limited of Matlock was donated by Mr Robert Shields, a former High Sheriff of Derbyshire.

325

MERCIAN WOOD

This is a mixed species woodland of individually dedicated trees.

Photo by Phil Nixon

324

Photo by Barry Turner

ROYAL TANK REGIMENT

The very first battle involving tanks took place on the Somme, when approximately 30 tanks attacked German positions between the villages of Flers and Courcelette on Friday 15 September 1916. This was one of the largest battles of World War I, with more than one million casualties. At dawn on 20 November 1917, the first successful tank battle was fought at Cambrai involving some 300 Mark IV tanks. The arrival of the tank signalled the end of trench warfare and established the tank as a dominant factor of battle right up to the present day.

The design of the Royal Tank Regiment grove reflects these events with a collection of Ash trees, a tree of significance to the Regiment, some of which have been propagated from trees from the battlefield at Cambrai, while inside the circular seat is an oak tree from the village of Flers Courcelette on the Somme. On the brick plinth is a model of a Mark IV, one of the earliest tanks. In the spring, the Grove bursts into colour with hundreds of daffodils planted in the pattern of tank tracks. On the flagpole flies the Regimental flag of brown, red and green signifying 'through mud and blood to green fields beyond.'

ROYAL CORPS OF SIGNALS

The Royal Signals Association (RSA) was formed in 1920 as the 'Royal Engineers Old Comrades Association Signals Branch.' The Association aims to provide comfort and relief to past and present signallers and their dependents who are in conditions of need, hardship or distress. It also exists to foster comradeship and morale within the Corps family, serving and retired. The RSA has 68 branches in the UK and 28 Unit Associations that are affiliated.

The Corps Memorial was unveiled by the Colonel in Chief, The Princess Royal, in May 2008. This is a statue depicting the cap badge of the Royal Corps of Signals which represents Mercury, messenger to the Gods. It has been given the nickname 'Jimmy' by the Corps.

No-one is certain how this nickname came about, one theory being that the figure is based upon a sculpture by Giambologna, an Italian, whose nickname was eventually shortened to Jimmy. More likely is that it followed the popularity of a member of the Corps Jimmy Emblem, who was the British Army Boxing champion in 1926!

326

Photo by Barry Turner

IRISH INFANTRY GROVE

In June 2000, the Archbishop of Armagh, Robin Eames, and many hundreds of members of the Irish Infantry Regiments gathered to dedicate this garden which is planted with trees native to Ireland. The grove includes Irish yews and an oak from a stand of oak in Tollymore Forest Park which was one of the few species in Ireland to have survived the last Ice Age.

The grove, with its memorial stone of Belfast black and Mourne granites, commemorates all the members of the Irish Infantry Regiments who have served the Crown since the raising of the original Royal Irish Regiment (18th) in 1684.

327

COMMANDER DAVID CHILDS' TREES

Two trees were planted to thank the founder of the Arboretum; one plaque reads: The Founder's Tree, "To be remembered is o'er paid".

Photo by OceanBarefoot

THE GOLDEN GROVE

This raised circular earthwork contains a planting of dedicated golden trees and shrubs to celebrate the lives of couples of the World War II generation who have been married for 50 years.

The taller trees of the innermost ring are Malus and Sorbus that bear golden fruit and these are surrounded by golden stemmed ash. The first tree in this grove was planted by HRH the Duke of Kent to celebrate the Golden Wedding Anniversary of HM The Queen and Prince Phillip. In the autumn of 1999, the Staffordshire Guides planted over 10,000 daffodil bulbs on the inside bank of the Golden Grove as their Millennium Project, making a glorious show each Spring.

Photo by Barry Turner

THE QUEEN ALEXANDRA'S ROYAL ARMY NURSING CORPS

Queen Alexandra's Imperial Military Nursing Service was founded in 1902, becoming Queen Alexandra's Royal Army Nursing Corps (QARANC) in 1949.

Its members have served in all theatres of war since formation. At the end of World War II there were 12,000 QAs, many of whom had experienced the horrors of the Far East, Italy and Northern Europe. QAs were present when the British Army relieved the concentration camp at Belsen.

The QA's most notable veteran, for her service both during and after the Second World War, was Brigadier Dame Margot Turner DBE RRC. Surviving a direct hit on the SS Kuala having been ordered to leave Singapore in February 1942 with other civilian and service women, she survived the shelling of two ships she was on before being captured. She then spent three and a half years as a prisoner of war of the Japanese. She continued her career in the QAs after the War and was promoted to Matron-in-Chief and Director Army Nursing Services in 1964.

The award of the Royal Red Cross and Associate Royal Red Cross to officers and soldiers reflects their devotion to duty. When not on operations, they provide primary and secondary care to servicemen and civilians.

Photo: copyright National Memorial Arboretum

POLISH FORCES WAR MEMORIAL

The memorial commemorates the Polish men and women who gave their lives in World War II. Polish Armed Forces veterans from across the UK joined guests including HRH The Duke of Kent, Her Excellency Barbara Krystyna Tuge-Erecińska, Ambassador of the Republic of Poland, senior figures from the UK and Polish governments and their Armed Forces, to dedicate the memorial on 10 September 2009.

The memorial is superbly located at the eastern end of The Beat. Four humble toy soldiers, each painted a bronze colour and glued back-to-back atop a two-penny piece provided the inspiration behind the memorial's design. The statue is set within an 18 metre diameter architectural feature which has a series of inset plaques describing the Polish contribution in World War II. The memorial was made in Poland – the four figures represent their army, navy, air force and underground movement. Incorporated within the statue is the symbol of the Polish Eagle (the Polish State emblem), uniting all four sculptures under its outspread wings. The feature was designed by London-based civil engineering and architectural services company, Soarbond Ltd.

During World War II, the Polish were the fourth largest fighting force on the Allied side. They were also instrumental in helping the Allies to crack the Enigma code as explained on the plaque on the wall. Even before 1939 there were two Poles working on the code and the underground fighters made sure all their notes came to Britain.

The memorial is designed to act not only as a tribute to the fallen, but also as an educational aid for those visitors not familiar with the history of the Allied Polish Forces.

ROYAL ARMY MEDICAL CORPS

This large woodland has red and gold leaved trees individually dedicated to members of the Royal Army Medical Corps (RAMC).

A memorial plinth stands at the entrance to a central avenue of purple leaved trees planted as a tribute to the 29 members who were awarded the Victoria Cross, two of them gaining the award twice (and one George Cross). HM Queen Elizabeth The Queen Mother was Colonel in Chief of the Corps and the RAMC planted a tree in the grove to commemorate her 100th birthday.

ROYAL ARMY DENTAL CORPS

The Army Dental Corps was formed on 11th January 1921. In recognition of their past services his Majesty the King, King George VI, granted the prefix Royal on 28th November 1946 thus forming the Royal Army Dental Corps. The corps motto is Ex Dentibus Ensis which means from the teeth a sword and is taken from the legend of Cadmus. In Greek mythology Cadmus slew a dragon that had killed his companions. On instructions from Athena he sowed the dragons' teeth in the ground and a race of fierce men sprang up called Sparti (Sown).

The Memorial Stone was originally placed outside the old Connaught Hospital Building Aldershot. The sole member of the RADC remembered as an individual is Sergeant "Geordie" Muldoon who was murdered in Northern Ireland in 1974. He is remembered in the Ulster Grove.

Photo by Phil Nixon

SHOT AT DAWN

During World War I, 306 British and Commonwealth soldiers were shot for desertion, cowardice, striking a senior officer, disobeying a lawful order, casting away arms and sleeping at post. Most of them were sentenced after a short trial at which no real opportunity for defence was allowed. Today, it is recognised that several of them were under age when they volunteered and that many of them were suffering from post traumatic stress disorder, not recognised as a medical condition until 1980.

Andy De Comyn's statue 'Shot at Dawn' is modelled on Private Herbert Burden, of the 1st Battalion Northumberland Fusiliers, who was shot at Ypres in 1915, aged 17.

The names of Herbert Burden and those others who suffered the fate of being shot at dawn are listed on the stakes arranged in the form of a Greek theatre around the statue, symbolising the tragedy that these events signify. Many of the posts say 'Age Unknown' and this is because many young men lied about their age in order to enlist. Some of them had no representation at court-martial because most of the officers had been killed when they went 'over the top' first. (The average life expectancy of an officer on the front line was 10 weeks).

Many visitors ask about the location of the memorial in the Arboretum. It seems appropriate that it should be on the eastern edge where dawn strikes first.

The six trees facing the posts represent the firing squad, all aiming for the medallion around the statue's neck and none of them knowing who had the fatal bullet. It must have been very traumatic for them too, having to shoot one of their own.

After the 75 year Secrecy Act was lifted, members of the Shot at Dawn Organisation started campaigning for pardons.

The campaign commenced in 1992 and was led by Janet Booth, who sought a pardon for her Grandfather, Private Harry Farr. Janet's grandmother had lived with the shame and stigma of her husband being shot for cowardice in 1916. She believed he was wrongly convicted and actually suffered from 'shellshock'. Harry Farr's family took the Ministry of Defence to the High Court and won. In 2006, a posthumous pardon was granted for Harry and the other men.

Photo by OceanBarefoot

LICHFIELD WOOD

The City of Lichfield Wood was sponsored by the Swinfen Broun Trust, a local charity.

The mix of native trees includes species relating to districts of the city such as The Cherry Orchard. The name Lichfield derives from an early English phrase meaning 'the clearing in the grey woods' and some of the trees here are native ones with grey bark. Many of the trees have been sponsored by local groups and individuals associated with, or living in, the Lichfield District area.

IN MEMORY OF
A KIND LADY DONOR
15th October 2011
Sincere gratitude from
a liver recipient and her
family.

Photo by Phil Nixon

ROYAL GLOUCESTERSHIRE, BERKSHIRE AND WILTSHIRE REGIMENT

This memorial commemorates the above Regiments.

The Royal Wiltshire Regiment (62nd / 99th) 1756 – 1959
The Royal Berkshire Regiment (49th / 66th) 1743 – 1959

From 1959 – 1994 these two regiments then became The Duke of Edinburgh's Royal Regiment 1959 – 1994 and The Gloucester Regiment (28th / 61st) 1694 – 1994

From 1994 – 2007 they became known as the Royal Gloucestershire, Berkshire & Wiltshire Regiment

From 2007 they became part of The Rifles.

Photo by Barry Turner

THE SHOWMEN'S GUILD OF GREAT BRITAIN

This unique memorial commemorates members of the Guild who have died during conflict. The Showmen's Guild of Great Britain is the trade association for the travelling funfair industry. It represents the 4,100 members who operate the majority of travelling funfairs throughout Great Britain and Northern Ireland. The 23,500 family members between them run over 100 fairs weekly throughout the year.

The Showmen's Guild members are, through their work in running fairs, responsible for raising thousands of pounds for local, regional and national charities.

James Albert Ryan, Showman from the Midland Section, was the original 'Private Ryan' from Walsall, whose experiences were the inspiration for the Tom Hanks / Stephen Spielberg 1998 Hollywood blockbuster. In reality, James was in the Tank Division of 30 Corps working on the dangerous task of mine clearance.

George Thompson, Showman from Blackpool, served in the D-Day Landings with HMS Dispatch and subsequently saw action across Europe including in France, the German Rhine and defending Holland's tidal dykes. Additionally, he was among those sent to relieve the victims of Auschwitz in Poland.

KINGFISHER WOOD

A mixed woodland of individually dedicated native trees, named after the kingfishers seen flying along the nearby river bank.

GCHQ MEMORIAL

This memorial commemorates all British and Allied personnel whose work with Signals Intelligence and Information Assurance has supported Her Majesty's Government in war and peace since 1914.

There are two engraved bands. One is in Morse Code, reading "GCCS – Government Code & Cipher School", and the other in binary reading "GCHQ – Government Communications Headquarters". The sculptor is Nick Johnson.

Photo by Phil Nixon

THE INTELLIGENCE CORPS

The work of the Corps and the Intelligence Department during World War I extended to all areas. The Corps successfully ran a number of agents behind enemy lines.

During World War II, signals intelligence developed beyond all recognition – for example, the importance of the teams who cracked the Enigma Code at Bletchley Park is now well known. The Corps played a prominent part in rounding up war criminals, such as the arrest of Heinrich Himmler.

In the latter half of the twentieth century, the Corps played a major role in the strategies of counter-espionage and intelligence that characterised the Cold War in Europe and Asia. Since World War II, the Corps has served alongside the British Army on all its major deployments.

The roses were specially commissioned for the memorial and are named after part of the Corps motto: "Cognitio".

Photo by Phil Nixon

BIRMINGHAM CHILDREN'S HOSPITAL

There are five sculptures along this Riverside Walk, as well as further pieces within Birmingham Children's Hospital. The organic or 'seed-like' sculptures represent the key sentiments of love, loss, endings and new beginnings. There is a bench at the beginning of the walk.

The artwork was designed in consultation with parents, children, young people and Birmingham Hospital Bereavement Care Team and crafted by artists Matthew Lane Sanderson and Jane Dorner.

331a

ARMY APPRENTICE NATIONAL MEMORIAL

The Army Apprentices served from 1923 to 2004 and trained more than 70,000 soldier tradesmen for a number of regiments and corps of the British Army.

Boys aged 14 to 17 joined the Army to serve apprenticeships at Apprentice Schools / Colleges before "passing out" to serve in the Regular Army as soldier/tradesmen. Later, as NCOs and officers, these men formed a nucleus of military and trade skills within their various regiments and corps.

The memorial consists of an engraved and polished granite monolith, carrying the Army Apprentices School badge, set on a circular granite base. A central raised engraved circular granite disc carries further text and a list of all apprentice schools. Commemorative tablets encircle the memorial and these were donated by ex-apprentices or their families.

The Army Apprentice National Memorial is dedicated to all the army apprentices who served their country and in memory of those who gave their lives for it.

Photo by Barry Turner

HOUSEHOLD DIVISION

On top of the stone plinth stands a copy of the railings from the old Chelsea barracks, and mounted on to them are the original five badges of the foot guards. On the rear of the plinth are the mottos of the five Regiments of Foot Guards in the Household Division.

The badges of the Household Cavalry are in the most senior positions on the memorial, out on the flanks, while the guards are placed in order of seniority, with the Grenadier Guards on the right flank, then the Scots Guards, the Welsh Guards and the Irish Guards with the Coldstream Guards on the left. These positions are as the Guards would have been placed facing the enemy, so look to be in reverse order when seen from the front.

The memorial is paved with coloured stones interlocking with each other. These stones have been taken from England (white granite), Scotland (red granite), Ireland (green limestone) and Wales (black slate). The stones represent the union of the regiments despite their rivalry.

Around the back of the memorial are five Wellingtonia trees, also known as Giant redwood or Giant sequoia. These trees were chosen because the Duke of Wellington had connections with The Guards during the Napoleonic Wars.

LIGHT INFANTRY MEMORIAL

This Portland stone monolith and adjacent benches, dedicated on 12 June 2011, are "In proud memory of all those who served in the Light Infantry". The eight Regiments whose names are carved on the seats all served as Light Infantry after the formation of the Light Infantry Group in 1946, although they were all granted the honour of the title Light Infantry in the 19th Century.

At one time the Light Infantry was the largest regiment of infantry in the British Army. In 2007, the Light Infantry became a constituent part, with the Royal Green Jackets and two other distinguished Regiments, of a new large regiment: The Rifles. They proudly retain the Bugle cap badge which features on the stone – the universal symbol of the founder regiments.

THE DURHAM LIGHT INFANTRY

This memorial is dedicated to all who served in the Regiment and in memory of those who also gave their lives in the cause of freedom. Their motto is 'Faithful'.

Montgomery of Alamein said, "There may be some regiments as good but I know of none better".

Photo by Phil Nixon

THE MALL

This area includes the following memorials:

Household Division REME

The Light Infantry

The Durham Light Infantry

The Parachute Regiment and Airborne Forces Memorial

Queens Dragoon Guards.

1ST THE QUEEN'S DRAGOON GUARDS

This memorial is dedicated to all who served, and in memory of those who gave their lives in the service of, their regiment and country.

- 1st The Queen's Dragoon Guards
- 1st King's Dragoon Guards
- The Queen's Bays (2nd Dragoon Guards)

The Queen's Bays are sometimes referred to as The Welsh Cavalry because they recruit from Wales and the English / Welsh border counties.

THE PARACHUTE REGIMENT AND AIRBORNE FORCES

This memorial was commissioned as a national memorial to all those who have served, it plays a focal role in Remembrance and the grieving of bereaved families.

The emblem of the Airborne Forces is Bellerophon mounted on the winged horse Pegasus. The first recorded instance of an airborne warrior, his exploits are recounted in Greek mythology, where he is chiefly famous for slaying the fire-breathing monster Chimera. Mounted on Pegasus, with spear in hand, Bellerophon rode into the air, swooped down upon the monster and destroyed it.

The memorial sculptors are Charlie Langton for Pegasus and Mark Jackson (son of General Sir Michael Jackson) for the human figures.

Photo by Barry Turner

ROYAL ELECTRICAL AND MECHANICAL ENGINEERS (REME)

The two badges at the side of the seat are their former badge and their current one. Future planting includes oak trees and bluebells: 'bluebell' was the Royal Electrical and Mechanical Engineers (REME) call sign.

The small memorial to the right remembers Lance Corporal Kevin 'Dinger' Bell from REME who was killed in Bosnia. It originally marked the spot in Bosnia where he died, but was brought back to the UK when troops pulled out.

ROYAL AIR FORCE WOOD

This is a woodland of mixed native trees alongside the River Tame dedicated to individuals who have served in the Royal Air Force and includes a tree dedicated to Wing Commander Guy Gibson VC of 'Dambusters' fame.

334

ROYAL AIR FORCE CRANWELL APPRENTICES

A Staffordshire blue brick plinth and memorial plaque, sponsored by the Royal Air Force Cranwell Apprentices Association in 2005, is dedicated to all aircraft apprentices who trained at Royal Air Force Cranwell from 1922 to 1952. Cranwell is currently the home of the Royal Air Force College.

335

ROYAL AIR FORCE BOY ENTRANTS

The RAF Boy Entrants memorial was dedicated on 11 September 2004 in memory of the many thousands of Boy Entrants who trained between 1934 and 1965 and to record their singular contribution to the Royal Air Force.

The memorial design includes a stone monolith carved by Viv Astling, sculptor and stone mason, who located the piece of 'Ancaster' hard white stone. The names of the 10 RAF Stations where Boy Entrants trained are mounted on the Staffordshire blue brick plinths.

336

COASTAL COMMAND

Founded on 14 July 1936, Coastal Command, with its motto "Constant Endeavour", was an organisation within the Royal Air Force which defended the United Kingdom from naval threats and countered German U-Boats from the air.

The memorial grove of the maritime variety of Corsican pine trees is dedicated to all who served in Coastal Command and Flying Boats, and is appropriately situated overlooking the water of the River Tame.

Photo by David Fann

RAF LOCKING

Apprentice training started at RAF Locking in 1952 and the accommodation, messing and medical facilities were all housed in wooden huts. Training facilities were, however, mostly brick-built hangars. The Aircraft Apprenticeship comprised a year of basic mental and physical training followed by two years of more specialised instruction. The apprenticeships covered the Ground Radar, Ground Wireless and Air Radio trades. During the mid 1960s, changes were made in the Apprentice Training system following the raising of the school leaving age from 15 to 16 and a two year apprenticeship was introduced and called the Craft Apprenticeship.

Successful graduates passed out as Corporals with ONC as opposed to Junior Technicians. In 1970, a one year course was introduced to be undertaken by Mechanic Apprentices but apprentice training finally finished in March 1976, ending 54 years of 'Trenchard's Brats'.

Photo by Phil Nixon

THE RAIL INDUSTRY

This memorial is in celebration of the magnificent achievements of the railway family which has served the British Isles with great distinction. It was commissioned by the British Transport Pensioners Association. A Class 8f locomotive, carved from matt black granite, rests on top of the plinth. It was originally designed in 1935 by William Stanier for the LMSR (London Midland and Scottish Railway). They were built between 1935 and 1946.

The rear displays a montage of artwork designed by a specialist railway artist depicting a series of railway activities etched into the black shiny granite plaque. Facing in a generally southerly direction allows sunlight to shine directly onto the montage.

GIRLS VENTURE CORPS

The Girls Venture Corps Air Cadets is a voluntary uniformed organisation set up to meet the aspirations of young women between the ages of 11 – 20 and adult volunteers of all ages. This is achieved by providing an aviation, adventure and travel-based programme of activities which include overseas visits and service to the community.

RAF ADMINISTRATIVE APPRENTICES

The memorial commemorates all who trained as RAF Administrative Apprentices and Apprentice Clerks from 1925 – 1973 at Ruislip, St. Athan, Hereford and Bircham Newton.

THE CHELTENHAM COLLEGE MEMORIAL

This commemorates the memory of former pupils who have served in wars and campaigns since 1841. The Victoria Cross was awarded to 14 former pupils.

WOMEN'S SECTION, THE ROYAL BRITISH LEGION

The stone plinth, surrounding garden and benches are dedicated to members and friends of The Royal British Legion Women's Section. The memorial was opened on the 6 June 2005 by their National President HRH The Princess Royal. The three trees in the garden are maple, mountain ash and a three stemmed silver birch.

Photo by Phil Nixon

Photo by Phil Nixon

ROYAL NATIONAL LIFEBOAT INSTITUTION

This memorial has been designed to reflect the work of Royal National Lifeboat Institution (RNLI) crews and the relationship between crew members, a rescued person and all their families whose lives become interwoven during a rescue. It is intended not only as a celebration and recognition of the work of the RNLI but also to honour those crew members and people who have lost their lives saving others.

The design was created by gardener and TV presenter Chris Beardshaw and is an enhancement of the original memorial that was designed and funded by local volunteers.

Chris Beardshaw has created a coastal scene – a beautiful space in which to contemplate and reflect on the work of the RNLI. It embodies the journey of one member of a volunteer crew. As you enter you'll see the statue of a lifeboat crew member, created by Andrew Fitchett. Take the path going to the left, and the colours of the plants are calm and muted like the sea on a calm day. The stone monoliths represent more crew members heading out on a rescue mission. As you pass by the groynes and beach, you overlook the water. The colours change to shades of red to embody danger and stormy waters. The stone cairn represents those rescued encircled by the crew and the last stone monolith on your journey symbolises the crews and survivors returning to safety and their families.

The memorial's aim is to encourage the visitor to reflect on the sacrifice given by those crew members who did not return.

Photo by Barry Turner

Through forty years of sterling service, the Shackleton Units of the Royal Air Force and the South African Air Force preserved the freedom of the sea and skies. This memorial is dedicated to all who served with them. 1951 to 1991

THE SHACKLETON ASSOCIATION

SHACKLETON ASSOCIATION MEMORIAL

The Avro Shackleton was in service with the RAF and the South African AF from 1951 to 1991. Known by many as the work horse of the Cold War, they were used in anti-submarine, maritime reconnaissance, air sea rescue and airborne early warning roles. During those forty years, 16 aircraft were lost with 150 fatalities. Patrols of fourteen hours were not uncommon, which stretched the endurance of the aircrews and the skill of the ground crews in keeping them airworthy.

The memorial was erected by the Shackleton Association and is dedicated to all who served with Shackleton squadrons and units.

338

THE 41 CLUB

The 41 Club is an association of past members of the Round Table – The National Association of Round Tables in Great Britain and Ireland.

Round Table was founded by Louis Marchesi, a Rotarian, in Norwich in 1927, for young men aged between 18 and 40. He was inspired by a speech by the then Prince of Wales who said "The young business and professional men of this country must get together round the table, adopt methods that have proved so sound in the past, adapt them to the changing needs of the times and wherever possible, improve them".

This memorial celebrates the community service achievements and the millions of pounds raised for charities by Round Tablers since then. It takes the form of a garden with 41 trees, surrounding an obelisk.

Originally Round Tablers had to retire at 40 (hence the name 41 Club), but in 1988 the age limit was raised to 45. This Garden was created by Lichfield 41 Club, following a national appeal to the Association of Ex-Round Tablers' Clubs – the 41 Club.

The sundial was provided by the Tangent Club.

Photo by OceanBarefoot

Photo by Barry Turner

ANCIENT BURIAL MOUND

This is a 3,000 year old Bronze Age burial mound and, because it is classed as a scheduled ancient monument, it cannot be planted with trees or built upon. The mound has not been quarried and is allowed to develop as a wildflower meadow, providing a haven for wildlife.

THE ROYAL OBSERVER CORPS

The Observer Corps, founded in 1925 to track aircraft, was a uniformed volunteer organisation that enjoyed a long association with the Royal Air Force. The badge of the Royal Observer Corps depicts a beacon lighter of Elizabethan times and the Corps motto, "Forewarned is Forearmed".

The Observer Corps was one of the cornerstones of Lord Dowding's air defence system during World War II. In 1941, HM King George VI conferred the title 'Royal' for the sterling service given by the Observer Corps during the Battle of Britain, and in September of that year women were enrolled in the Corps. In 1944, some 796 members of the Observer Corps volunteered to man the Defensively Equipped Merchant Ships during the D-Day Landings. Three members lost their lives on board.

During the Cold War, the Corps was given a nuclear reporting role. In 1995, the decision was finally taken to stand-down the remaining elements of the Corps, completing 70 years of outstanding voluntary service at the forefront of the defence of the realm.

Photo by Phil Nixon

II (ARMY COOPERATION) SQUADRON

No II Squadron was formed at Farnborough on 13 May 1912 as one of the original Squadrons of the Royal Flying Corps. After training on a number of types of aircraft, it moved to France in August 1914 as part of the British Expeditionary Force and later standardised on BE 2s. Flying from many locations in France during World War I, the Squadron provided the vital reconnaissance information needed by our ground forces on the Western Front.

The Squadron has been deployed in many of the arenas of war since World War I and celebrated its 100th Anniversary on the 13 May 2012: the first and thus the oldest fixed wing Squadron in the world, with a record of service that is truly 'Second to None'.

The Squadron was awarded two VCs during World War I, 2Lt Rhodes-Moorhouse and 2Lt Alan MacLeod, a Canadian pilot serving with the Squadron.

RAF BENEVOLENT FUND

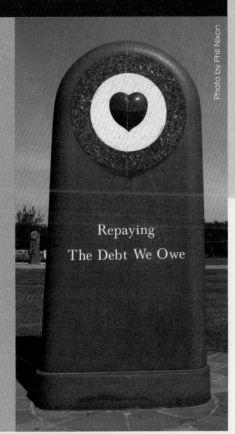

Photo by Phil Nixon

Repaying The Debt We Owe

The Royal Air Force Benevolent Fund has a proud tradition of looking after its own. The RAF Benevolent Fund is the RAF's leading welfare charity and is an extension of that tradition. Since its foundation in 1919, it has supported the RAF family and provided a spectrum of care, supporting everyone from children growing up on RAF stations and those serving today to keep our skies safe, to the veterans who fought for our freedom.

They are an independent charity, receiving no government funding, supporting the RAF Memorial in London, the RAF family and the morale and wellbeing of the serving RAF.

Winston Churchill said, "The RAF Benevolent Fund is part of the conscience of the British nation."

Photo by Barry Turner

ROYAL AIR FORCES ASSOCIATION REMEMBRANCE GARDEN

The first national Remembrance Garden in memory of all those who have served in the RAF and Commonwealth air forces was opened by HRH The Princess Royal on Monday 28 September 2009.

The inspiration for the Remembrance Garden comes from the RAF Association's Dedication, the last line of which is "we will remember them". The central feature of the 50 metre-long garden is the RAF Association emblem – a magnificent stainless steel eagle sitting on top of a globe. The eagle, named Winston, is made up of over 1,000 hand-forged feathers and is surrounded by a segmented RAF roundel separated into four quarters to depict the RAF Association at the heart of RAF welfare.

The RAF Association Remembrance Garden will preserve the memory of serving and ex-serving members of the RAF for many years to come. Relatives, friends and colleagues of anyone who has served in the RAF will be able to create a permanent memorial by planting an individual cross in the garden in memory of their loved one.

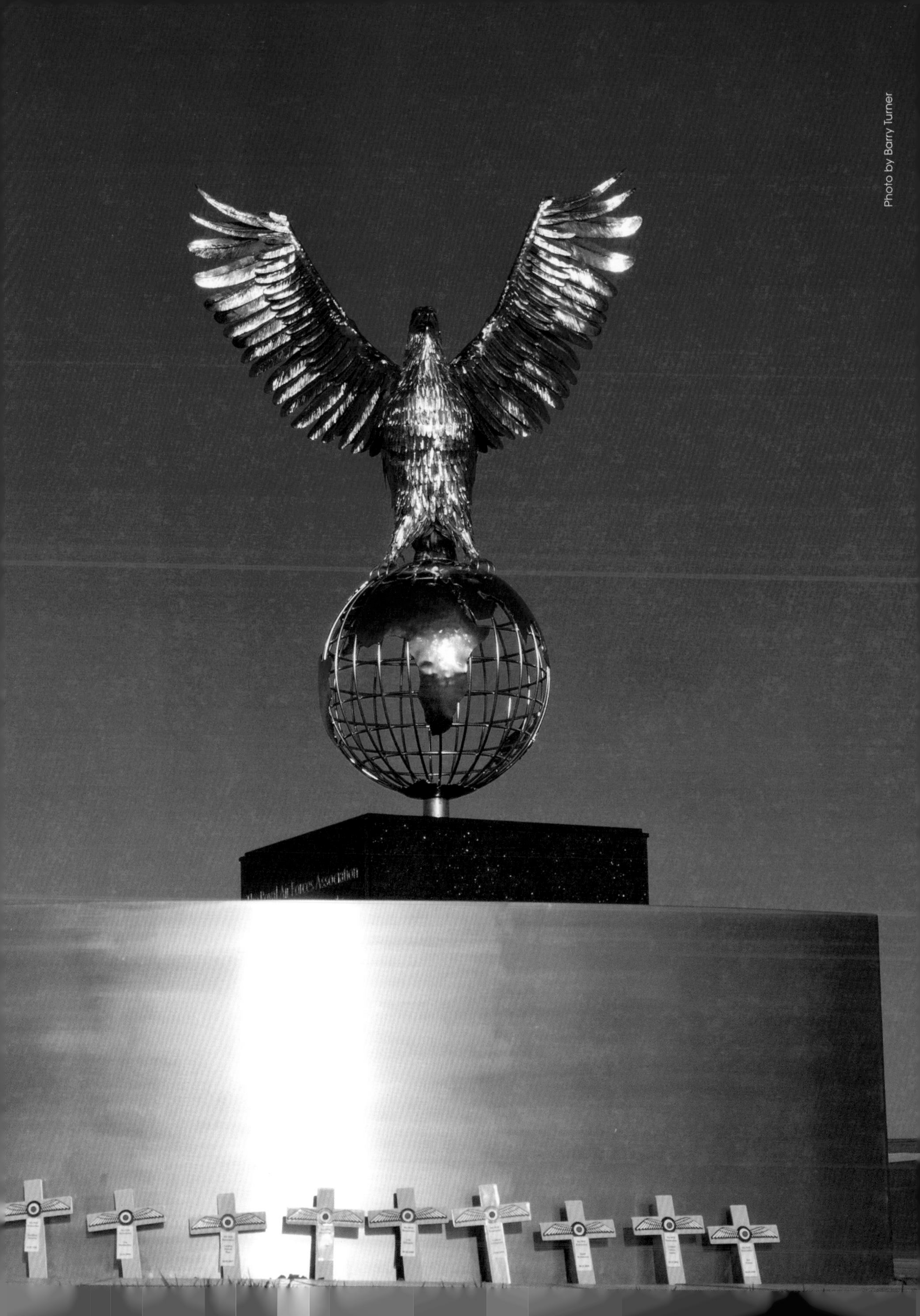

Photo by Barry Turner

ROYAL & SUN ALLIANCE MEMORIALS

Photo by Barry Turner

Two large carved memorials complete the collection of memorial plaques displayed on the wooden walls of the Cloisters.

The memorials are from insurance companies that have amalgamated with other companies and moved to new premises. These elegant memorials remember members of their staff who served and fell during the two World Wars.

NO 30 SQUADRON ASSOCIATION

On 10 September 2008, No 30 Squadron Association dedicated the first memorial at the Arboretum to a current flying Squadron. No 30 Squadron Association was formed in 1985 under the Chairmanship of Air Vice Marshal David Dick, who had served on Thunderbolts in Burma. He was also the test pilot who intentionally put the Javelin aircraft into a spin to explore why it happens and to find a procedure to help pilots recover from a spin.

From its formation in Egypt in 1915 to its present role as part of the Brize Norton Transport Wing, No 30 Squadron has always justified its motto "Ventre a terre", translated as "Flat Out". The Squadron pioneered the dropping of supplies to beleaguered troops in Mesopotamia in World War I and was instrumental in devising an aerial policing policy during the inter-war period. In Greece during World War II, 30 Squadron's Blenheims took part in many raids on the advancing enemy before being forced to retreat. After re-grouping, the Squadron served in Ceylon (now Sri Lanka) and India and, during the latter stages of the war, in a fighter-bomber role in Burma. In the late 1940s, the Squadron took on its present role of air transportation, participating in the Berlin Airlift and progressing from Dakotas through Valettas and Beverleys to its present aircraft, the C130 Hercules; first the 'K' model and now the Hercules 'J'. The Hercules has flown in all recent major operations including the Falklands, the Gulf Wars, the Balkans, Iraq, and now in Afghanistan. Every Humanitarian Relief Operation around the world has seen 30 Squadron crews participating. The Squadron's Battle Honours are engraved on the reverse side of the memorial.

ROYAL AIR FORCE SERVICING COMMANDO AND TACTICAL SUPPLY WING ASSOCIATION

The avenue of 16 maple trees, dedicated bench and memorial plinth is a tribute to the RAF Servicing Commandos.

In January 1942, a memo signed by Louis Mountbatten was sent from the War Cabinet Annex to the Air Ministry proposing the formation of RAF Servicing Commandos. World War II Commando Units were trained along similar lines to the Army and Royal Marine Commandos, supervised by the Army. Training was followed by amphibious exercises at the Combined Training Centre at Inveraray.

Units operated in Normandy and the Continent, India, Burma, Indo-China (Saigon) and Java, North Africa, Sicily and Italy.

ROYAL AUXILIARY AIR FORCE

Photo by Barry Turner

The impressive brick memorial topped with a large antique metal cast of an eagle is to commemorate all who served in the Royal Auxiliary Air Force (RAuxAF).

The memorial and surrounding trees were dedicated in September 2004 by HRH the Duke of Gloucester. The RAuxAF was formed in 1924 to provide a reserve of part-time volunteers who could be called upon to support the RAF during times of need. The squadrons served with distinction during World War II, especially during the Battle of Britain, were re-formed in 1946 and largely disbanded in 1957 but have since been revived, with some 20 units currently in existence.

343a

AIRCREW ASSOCIATION MEMORIAL

The memorial consists of a Mountsorrell red granite rough hewn stone displaying the propeller logo.

The Aircrew Association was founded on 8 September 1977 to foster comradeship amongst aircrew who had been awarded a military flying badge.

344

ROYAL CANADIAN AIR FORCE

Military aviation in Canada began in 1914, but it was not until 1917 that Canada had a professional Air Force. In 1918, the Air Ministry decided to form two Canadian Squadrons, one fighter and one day bomber squadron, and soon approved the formation of the Canadian Air Force.

The post war Air Force was unique, as most of its work was civilian in nature, mapping, pioneering new air routes, carrying mail, suppressing smuggling and patrolling fishing grounds, so it was not until 1935 that the Royal Canadian Air Force resumed military operations, forming bomber and fighter squadrons three years later.

The monument is constructed from 3 blocks of solid granite, mortared together in the order of red, grey and red to represent the Canadian flag. The top of the memorial has a maple leaf that casts a shadow on the stone slabs, significantly to align with the 11 o'clock position on the 11th hour of the 11th month annually.

Photo by Phil Nixon

ROYAL AIR FORCE WING

The RAF memorial grove (RAF Wing) comprises a collection of silver birch trees planted in the shape of an eagle's wings. The wing honours both the Fighter and Bomber Commands. The trees are individually dedicated to some of the Squadrons. The central 'three bladed propeller' made up of dwarf golden honeysuckle plants was sponsored by the Aircrew Association. The grove also includes the following memorials:

- Princess Mary's RAF Nursing Service
- RAF 214 Squadron
- Second Tactical Air Force Memorial
- Flt Lt. J. W. Lucas DFC
- RAF No. 31 Squadron Memorial
- RAF Loadmasters' Association
- The Air Formation Squadron Crescent RAF
- RAF Medical Services
- RAF Search & Rescue

Photo by Barry Turner

THE ROYAL AIR FORCE POLICE

The Royal Air Force (RAF) Police have been supporting worldwide RAF operations since 1918. Peaking in 1945, the branch comprised 20,500 personnel and by 1948, RAF Police investigators had brought to justice the surviving killers of 50 RAF officers who had taken part in the Great Escape.

HM King George VI approved the RAF Police badge & motto in 1950 and throughout the 30 year 'Cold War' the branch provided security protection for the RAF's nuclear deterrent. Having served in 66 countries since 1918, the RAF Police are today in the forefront of the war against terrorism, serving in current conflicts. The RAF Police Association was formed in 1984. The RAF nickname for their police is 'Snowdrops' because they wear white hats, and this is reflected in the flowers engraved on the edges of the stone.

WOMEN'S AUXILIARY AIR FORCE (WAAF)

The Women's Auxiliary Air Force memorial represents their badge with the King's Crown emblem.

The cut-out letters on the upper roundel record all the important roles that the young women carried out between 1939 and 1945. The light passes through these words on to the plinth below and the words are seen as 'shadows of remembrance' in memory of those who lost their lives.

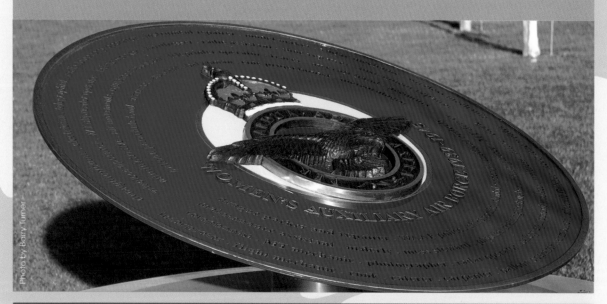

Photo by Barry Turner

AIR FORMATION AND AIR SUPPORT SIGNALS

By the end of World War II, some 21,000 soldiers, predominantly members of the Royal Corps of Signals, provided communications for Royal Air Force bases overseas.

The crescent of ten copper beech and maple trees remembers soldiers who have provided communications for the Royal Air Force from October 1917 to the present day. In all military operations and natural disasters they are among the vanguard, first in and last out. Three detachments landed in Normandy on D-Day and at present they provide communications for the Joint Helicopter Force in Afghanistan.

90 SIGNALS UNIT

90 Signals Unit (90SU) provides a vital role in ensuring the RAF achieves operational success and exists to provide Expeditionary Information Services, whenever they are required.

Comprising two Wings, Force Generation Wing (FGW) and Tactical Communications Wing (TCW), the Unit's history can be traced back to the mid 1950s, although TCW did not become an autonomous signals unit until later (1973). Since this time, 90SU have been involved in every major conflict and operation that has taken place worldwide.

Photo by Barry T

ROYAL AUSTRALIAN AIR FORCE

In line with the lime trees of Millennium Avenue are eucalyptus trees planted to represent local associations with 463 / 467 Squadrons Royal Australian Air Force.

ADJUTANT GENERAL'S CORPS COMMEMORATIVE GARDEN

The Adjutant General's Corps was formed on 6 April 1992 and is one of the largest Corps in the British Army. The Corps is comprised of four branches and provides combat human resources specialists, Military Police, Military Provost Staff, Military Provost Guard service, educational and training services and Army legal services. Representatives of the Corps serve in every unit of the British Army.

The commemorative garden design is based on a concept representing Winchester Cathedral, looking at and through the Cathedral's west elevation.

Walk through the tall trees at the entrance, which represent the portals of the west face of the Cathedral. The trees planted on the left and right represent the pillars either side of the main aisle, which in turn lead to the line of trees at the rear of the garden, symbolic of the high screen.

STAFFORDSHIRE REGIMENT

The Staffords are an amalgamation of two famous and much loved Regiments, The South Staffordshire Regiment which was formed in 1705 in Lichfield, and The North Staffordshire Regiment which was formed in 1756. Both Regiments distinguished themselves in campaigns all over the world. In World War I they fought in all the main battles including Mons, Loos, Somme and Ypres. In World War II, Staffordshire Battalions took part in heavy fighting in Dunkirk, Burma, Italy, Normandy and Arnhem.

The Regiments amalgamated in 1959, and the Staffords served in the Ugandan Mutiny, Northern Ireland, the Gulf War, Kosovo and two tours in Iraq. They now form the 3rd Battalion The Mercian Regiment.

Famous people from the Staffords include L/Cpl William Coltman VC, DCM & Bar, MM & Bar, one of the most highly decorated soldiers of World War I, who is remembered by an oak tree at the centre of the memorial.

Photo by Barry Turner

ASSOCIATION OF JEWISH EX-SERVICEMEN AND WOMEN

Made from Chinese granite and designed to give you a different perspective when viewed from different angles, the Star of David memorial by sculptor Harry Seager is dedicated to all members of the Jewish community who over the years have served Crown and country, and to the many who lost their lives in that service.

Photo by Barry Turner

Photo by Barry Turner

THE SHRIEVALTY AVENUE

Millennium Avenue incorporates a number of lime trees sponsored by High Sheriffs, some of whom were in office at the time of the Millennium.

All these trees were propagated from the 2,000 year-old lime tree growing at Westonbirt Arboretum in Gloucestershire. This Millennium sponsorship by High Sheriffs was singularly appropriate given that the office of High Sheriff (or Shire Reeve) is at least 1,000 years old, having its roots in Saxon times, well before the Norman Conquest of 1066. It is the oldest continuous secular office under the Crown. Originally a High Sheriff had vested in him many of the powers now vested in a Lord Lieutenant, High Court Judges and Magistrates. The office of High Sheriff remained first in precedence in the counties until King Edward VII, by Order in Council in 1908, gave that primacy to the Lord Lieutenant. The High Sheriff remains the Sovereign's representative in a county for all matters relating to the Judiciary and to the maintenance of law and order. The involvement of the High Sheriffs in the Millennium Avenue underlines their service to their Sovereign and to the counties for more than a thousand years.

GALLIPOLI

This memorial remembers the terrible loss of life which occurred during World War I when a force which famously included the Australian and New Zealand Army Corps (ANZAC) attempted to land and defeat the armies of the Ottoman Empire. They were attempting to capture Constantinople and secure a sea route to Russia. There were huge casualties on both sides.

The monument includes a tree sculpture of dead oak trees, pollarded to represent the arms and hands of injured soldiers reaching upwards in hope of rescue as they lay in the mud among the unburied dead.

Photo by Barry Turner

MERCIAN VOLUNTEERS

The Mercian Volunteers Regimental Association created the Mercian Grove in 2004 with four oak saplings and a stone memorial. It commemorates all those regular and Territorial Army (TA) soldiers who served with Mercian Volunteers and its constituent units between 1967 and 1988.

For 21 years, its battalions were part of the British Army's contribution to NATO during the Cold War and had a specific role in Germany. Its direct successor is the 4th Battalion The Mercian Regiment. Pte Luke Cole, one of its TA soldiers, was awarded the MC in 2007 whilst serving in Afghanistan.

HOME SERVICE FORCE

The memorial plinth with its surrounding trees, shrubs and plaques is dedicated to the HSF 1985 – 1992. The HSF was formed on 1 April 1985 as part of the Territorial Army (TA), although it is acknowledged that some units were formed on a trial basis earlier than this. Membership of the Home Service Force (HSF) was restricted to those who had previous service in the Armed Forces, or in the TA. 48 units were formed throughout the Country with each unit being attached to an existing Regular Army or TA, Regiment or Battalion for things such as administration and training.

The HSF was given the task of guarding key installations in the United Kingdom such as major power stations and communication centres, the loss of which through subversive enemy action could have seriously affected the running of the Country. However, in 1992 the threat that had necessitated the forming of HSF was considered to have diminished sufficiently to enable it to be disbanded.

Photo by Barry Turner

Photo by Barry Turner

TOC H

The name comes from a rest house for soldiers at Poperinge in Belgium, about six miles from Ypres. Open from 1915 to the end of World War I it was run by Rev. 'Tubby' Clayton, an Australian and a very jovial character.

The home was given the name Talbot House (TH = Toc H) in memory of Lieutenant Gilbert Talbot, killed in action, the brother of Rev Talbot who first had the idea for a rest home. It was open to all ranks, but rank had to be 'left at the door' because all men were equal once inside.

It became very popular, a haven of peace and safety away from the fighting, but was also described as "a lively pub without beer", and a chapel was built upstairs.

The famous lamp is an oil lamp used by Tubby Clayton. They do not give out much light, hence the saying "Dim as a Toc H lamp", meaning not too clever. It is now called 'The Lamp of Maintenance'. In the chapel you will find a replica of the lamp.

Post World War I, Toc H adopted the lamp as its symbol and the principles of fellowship, service, fair-mindedness and reconciliation. Branches existed in many countries around the world. Over the years it has followed its mission of healing the divisions of society through bringing people together and creating friendships between individuals.

THE BLUE ZONE

Access: From Far East Walk and Millennium Avenue.

Terrain: Firm surface on Yeomanry Avenue and Millennium Avenue with rough mown grassland around and between the memorials and trees.

Starting point: Intersection of Far East Walk and Yeomanry Avenue.

No	Memorial	Pg
401	YEOMANRY AVENUE	129
401a	BRITISH SOUTH AFRICA POLICE	129
401b	NYASALAND POLICE MEMORIAL	130
402	ROYAL HONG KONG POLICE	130
402a	NORTHERN RHODESIA POLICE MEMORIAL	130
403	BIDADARI CEMETERY	131
403a	MEMORIAL FOR ST JOHN VOLUNTEERS	131
404	BLESMA EXTENSION	131
405	YANGTZE INCIDENT	132
406	ROYAL INDIAN NAVY AND INDIAN ARMY	133
407	FAR EAST AIR FORCE	133
408	DIAMOND GROVE	133
409	ROYAL NORWEGIAN NAVY	134
409a	NATIONAL ASSOCIATION OF MEMORIAL MASONS	134
410	FLEET AIR ARM	135
410a	ROYAL MARINES ASSOCIATION	136
411	BRITISH NUCLEAR TEST VETERANS	136
411a	THE COMMANDOS	137
411b	SHROPSHIRE YEOMANRY MEMORIAL PLINTH	138
411b	STAFFORDSHIRE YEOMANRY	138
412	SOUTH ATLANTIC MEDAL ASSOCIATION MEMORIAL AND THE ANTELOPE GARDEN	139
413	ROYAL NAVAL REVIEW	141
413a	ROYAL NAVAL PATROL SERVICE	143
414	DEFENSIVELY EQUIPPED MERCHANT SHIPS	144
415	MASTER MARINERS SUNDIAL	144
416	THE MERCHANT NAVY CONVOY WOOD	145
416	THE MERCHANT NAVY ASSOCIATION MEMORIAL	146
416a	ROYAL FLEET AUXILIARY SHIP 'SIR PERCIVALE' ANCHOR	146
417	WOMEN'S ROYAL NAVAL SERVICE	147
417	THE VOLUNTARY AID DETACHMENT (RN)	148
417	HMS BARHAM	148
417	RUSSIAN CONVOY VETERANS	148
417a	ARMY DOG UNIT (NORTHERN IRELAND) ASSOCIATION RED PAW	149
417b	THE QUEEN ALEXANDRA'S ROYAL NAVAL NURSING SERVICE AND THE VOLUNTARY AID DETACHMENT (RN)	149
418	ULSTER SPECIAL CONSTABULARY	150
418a	THE ROYAL BRITISH LEGION NEVER FORGET TRIBUTE GARDEN	150
419	ARMED SERVICES WOOD	151
419	LIONS CLUB INTERNATIONAL – WOODEN SHELTER	151
419a	DOUGLAS SKENE GROVE	151
420	THE ULSTER ASH GROVE	152
420	THE ULSTER DEFENCE REGIMENT CGC	152
420a	THE RUC GC WAY	153
421	THE HOME FRONT	153
421a	THE NATIONAL EX-PRISONER OF WAR ASSOCIATION	154
422	THE CHILDREN'S WOODLAND / ACTIVITY AREA	155
422a	THE EDWARD'S TRUST GARDEN	156
423	FELLOWSHIP OF THE SERVICES	156
424	MILLENNIUM WOOD	156
424a	WOMEN'S INSTITUTE	157
424a	THE SALVATION ARMY	157
424a	YMCA	158
424a	COMBINED OPERATIONS COMMAND MEMORIAL	158
425	THE ROYAL BRITISH LEGION POPPY FIELD	159
425a	THE SPIRITUALISTS' NATIONAL UNION	159
425b	QUAKER SERVICES MEMORIAL	160
426	RAC FUTURE FORESTS	161
427	THE ROADPEACE WOOD	161
428	ALLIED SPECIAL FORCES ASSOCIATION GROVE	162
429	WESTERN FRONT ASSOCIATION MEMORIAL	163
430	UNITED NATIONS AVENUE	163
430	THE FORESTERS FRIENDLY SOCIETY	163
431	WATERSMEET	164

"THANK YOU FOR A BRILLIANT DAY. WE ALL REALLY ENJOYED IT. THE EDUCATION TEAM ARE DOING AN AMAZING JOB."
Doxey Primary School.

YEOMANRY AVENUE

This is an avenue of 48 large and small leaved lime trees where each tree is dedicated to a Yeomanry Unit.

In the 1790s, the threat of invasion of the Kingdom of Great Britain was high after the French Revolution and the rise of Napoleon Bonaparte. In order to improve the country's defences, volunteer regiments were raised in many counties from yeomen. The word 'yeoman' refers to small farmers who owned the land they cultivated, but the officers were drawn from the nobility and many of the men were their tenants. Yeomanry were not obliged to serve overseas without their individual consent.

During the first half of the 19th Century, Yeomanry Regiments were used extensively in support of the civil authority to quell riots and civil disturbances (including the Peterloo Massacre), but as police forces took over this role, the Yeomanry concentrated on local defence.

During the Boer War, companies of The Imperial Yeomanry were formed from volunteers from the Yeomanry to serve overseas. In 1908, the Yeomanry became part of the Territorial Army.

Photo by Phil Nixon

Photo by Barry Turner

BRITISH SOUTH AFRICA POLICE

This regimental memorial replicates that which was erected in 1921 in the Morris Depot (the training depot for new recruits) in Salisbury, Rhodesia (now Harare, Zimbabwe). This was originally known as the Blatherwick Memorial, Jimmy Blatherwick being the most famous Regimental Sergeant Major, who died in 1918.

The British South Africa Police (BSAP) was the Police Force of the British South Africa Company founded by Cecil Rhodes in 1889 to provide protection for the settlers. It became the Police Force of Southern Rhodesia (subsequently Rhodesia and now Zimbabwe).

The memorial was dedicated on 25 July 2010 and remembers all those who served in the British South Africa Police Force.

401b

NYASALAND POLICE MEMORIAL

Interred in this memorial is a scroll containing the names of officers who served in the Nyasaland Police from 1921 – 1964.

402

ROYAL HONG KONG POLICE

The Hong Kong Police Force was founded in 1844, when Hong Kong Island was ceded to Britain by China following the First Opium War.

The first Police Officers were European and Indian ex-soldiers, together with some locally recruited Chinese. In 1845, Charles May, a former London Metropolitan Police Superintendent, took command of the 171-strong Force. Hong Kong grew in importance as a trading port and, following the Japanese Occupation during World War II, also as a manufacturing, financial and tourist centre. The Force was honoured with the title 'Royal' following very serious disturbances arising from the Cultural Revolution which took place in China in 1967. By 1997, when sovereignty of Hong Kong returned to China, the population of Hong Kong was some 6.5 million people, and the Force consisted of 28,000 regular Police Officers, with 5,700 Auxiliaries and 6,000 civilian staff.

402a

NORTHERN RHODESIA POLICE MEMORIAL

This memorial commemorates all who served in the Northern Rhodesia Police from 1911 to 1964 and its predecessors the North Eastern Rhodesia Constabulary and Barotse Native Police, who suppressed the slave trade.

It particularly remembers those who died on duty in Northern Rhodesia (now Zambia) or on active service in East Africa 1914 – 1918.

The memorial consists of a black granite stone on a light grey honed granite plinth with an incised silver line map and solid gilded area showing Northern Rhodesia.

Photo by Barry Turner

403

BIDADARI CEMETERY

The four cherry trees commemorate the Bidadari Christian Cemetery, which contains the graves of people who died in Singapore from 1908 to 1972. Today, Bidadari Cemetery is no longer in use, and most of the graves have been exhumed to allow land redevelopment.

Photo by Phil Nixon

404

BLESMA EXTENSION

The 70 fruit trees – of varieties Bramley Seedling, Fiesta, James Grieve, Golden Delicious, Cox's Orange Pippin, Katie and Egremont Russet – are dedicated to the service personnel of the British Limbless Ex-Service Men's Association (BLESMA).

403a

Photo by Barry Turner

MEMORIAL FOR ST JOHN VOLUNTEERS

The garden has been designed to commemorate the thousands of volunteers who have helped the charity over the years in its mission to provide first aid in many different situations.

The Duke of Gloucester, who is the Grand Prior of the Order of St John, officially opened the memorial in 2009. The design of the memorial takes the form of the St John (Amalfi) Cross. The entrance is through one of the arms of the cross which is flanked by two granite panels depicting the badge of St John and the Priory of England and the Islands. At the centre of the cross is a black granite stone with the inscription: "In honour of all those who have faithfully served the Venerable Order of the Hospital of St John of Jerusalem and its foundations."

"YANGTZE INCIDENT GROVE."

Commemorating
The loss of our 46 shipmates
Yangtze River April 1949

"WE WILL REMEMBER THEM"

HMS CONSORT

HMS AMETHYST

In memory of our 21 Shipmates killed in 1949

Photo by Barry Turner

405

YANGTZE INCIDENT

The circular planting of 46 Chinese euonymus plants commemorates each life lost during the Yangtze Incident in China in 1949.

A plaque alongside the memorial tells the full story of the Yangtze Incident. Inside the circle are a black polished granite monument and trees planted as a tribute to HMS Amethyst, HMS Black Swan, HMS Consort and HMS London which were the four ships involved in the incident. The human cost in the four ships was 46 dead and 68 injured. The tree planted just outside the circle remembers the RAF Sunderland flying boat, named D-DOG ML772, from 88 Squadron that, on the fourth attempt, landed successfully on the Yangtze River alongside HMS Amethyst to deliver medical supplies and a replacement doctor.

406

Photo by Barry Turner

1746   1947

INDIAN ARMY

IN MEMORY OF THOSE WHO SERVED IN THE ARMED FORCES
OF THE HONORABLE EAST INDIA COMPANY FROM 1746 TO 1857
AND THE CROWN FROM 1857 TO 1947

H E I C

THEY SERVED IN CAMPAIGNS IN VARIOUS PARTS OF THE WORLD.
ALL VOLUNTEERS, THEY ENLISTED 1,500,000 MEN
IN WORLD WAR 1 AND OVER 2,500,000 IN WORLD WAR II.

ROYAL INDIAN NAVY AND INDIAN ARMY

Between the Yangtze Incident and Far East Air Force memorials, trees from the Indian sub-continent such as Kashmir rowan, cedar and Bhutan pine have been planted as a tribute to those who served in the Royal Indian Navy (1934 – 1947) and Indian Army. The British Indian Army (1858 – 1947) was a force recruited locally during the British Colonisation of India and commanded by British and Indian officers.

407

FAR EAST AIR FORCE

Dedicated in 2006, this memorial comprising 42 hand engraved Lakeland slate tiles commemorates the history of the Royal Air Force from 1948 to 1971, when the RAF was engaged in assisting the Malays through confrontation and a period of emergency.

Malaysia gained independence in 1957 and Singapore separated from Malaysia in 1965. As both nations developed their own Armed Forces, the RAF reduced its commitment and withdrew in 1971.

The Units listed on the memorial were the backbone of operations and provided bases for strategic reinforcement to the Far East, should it have been required.

Photo by Barry Turner

408

DIAMOND GROVE

The trees in the Diamond Grove have been sponsored by couples from the World War II generation to celebrate 60 years of marriage, their Diamond Wedding anniversary.

Photo by Barry Turner

ROYAL NORWEGIAN NAVY

This avenue holds native species of silver birch trees from Norway together with memorial plaques, all sponsored by the Royal Norwegian Navy and commemorating Norway's important involvement in protecting the Merchant Convoys of World War II.

Photo by Barry Turner

NATIONAL ASSOCIATION OF MEMORIAL MASONS

The Association was formed in 1907 to promote excellence and craftsmanship within the memorial masonry trade. Through its strict codes of business practice and working practice, the National Association of Memorial Masons (NAMM) demands the very highest standards of its members.

The NAMM exhibition was created to provide a permanent marker to celebrate 100 years of service to both its members and bereaved families. It is a timeline of memorialisation from Stone Age to the present day. The garden also aims to encourage children to understand how history, remembrance and heritage are linked to memorialisation.

The exhibition, designed as a Centenary Garden, was officially opened by HRH The Princess Royal on 20 May 2008.

FLEET AIR ARM

In 2009, the Royal Navy celebrated the Centenary of Naval Aviation and the memorial honours the sacrifice made by the 6,749 men and women who gave their lives in the service of naval aviation over the preceding 100 years.

Over 80% of front line Fleet Air Arm Squadrons are currently deployed on operations around the world, including Afghanistan. The memorial is a sculptured plinth of Portland stone supporting a granite aircraft carrier.

Photo by Phil Nixon

Where our Nation remembers

IN COMMEMORATION OF ALL RANKS OF
THE ROYAL MARINES
WHO HAVE LOST THEIR LIVES ON ACTIVE SERVICE
WE WILL REMEMBER THEM

Photo by Barry Turner

ROYAL MARINES ASSOCIATION

This memorial is of Dartmoor granite to represent the one part of the country that most Royal Marines will associate with their training. The Corps were founded in 1755 but their origins can be traced back to 1664. Many brave men and their families are remembered in this reflective place.

Any family that wishes to place a brass plaque on the benches so that a loved one is remembered by name can do so through the Royal Marines Association.

Photo by Phil Nixon

BRITISH NUCLEAR TEST VETERANS

Formed in 1983, the Association is a focus for the men who served at the test sites and combines comradeship with the objective of recognition of the ill effects suffered by some veterans.

Beginning in 1952 and continuing until 1965 there were 21 major British nuclear tests and numerous minor tests at the sites listed on the memorial. The Association has about 1,400 members of which one third are widows. Membership is limited to men who served, their widows and their descendants.

THE COMMANDOS

The British Commandos were first formed by the Army in June 1940 during World War II as a well-armed but non-regimental raider force, employing unconventional and irregular tactics to assault, disrupt and reconnoitre the enemy in mainland Europe and Scandinavia.

Initially raids were made by comparatively small numbers, were of short duration and at night, later growing in complexity and size. The Commandos were formed and operated in secrecy and produced a demoralising effect on German coastal forces while achieving celebrity status among the British public, comparable with that attached to fighter pilots, and shrouded in myth.

This memorial consists of a reproduction of part of the Association badge – the wreath in copper and the Fairbairn-Sykes fighting knife in stainless steel. The impressive piece was created at Anwick Forge in Lincolnshire and dedicated in the presence of HRH Prince Philip, The Duke of Edinburgh, in July 2007.

At the centre of the memorial is a stone with the names of 8 commandos awarded the Victoria Cross. Behind the memorial is a roll of honour listing all 1205 commandos who died in training or on operations during World War II.

SHROPSHIRE YEOMANRY MEMORIAL PLINTH

The memorial was dedicated on Saturday 13 March 2010 by Colonel Evans, President of the Association. It was built by Bob Sadler after a buy-a-brick scheme organised with Association members to raise funds. The central plaque was produced by stone mason John Beer.

Private Harold Whitfield VC

"On 10 March 1918 at Buji El Lisaneh, Egypt, during the first of three counter-attacks made by the enemy on the position which had just been captured by his battalion, Private Whitfield single-handedly charged and captured a Lewis gun, killed the whole gun team and turned the gun on the enemy, driving them back with heavy casualties. Later he organised and led a bombing attack on the enemy, again inflicting many casualties, and by establishing his party in their position saved many lives and materially assisted in the defeat of the counter-attack."

Photo by Phil Nixon

STAFFORDSHIRE YEOMANRY

In memory of all those who served in the Boer War (1900 – 1901) and World Wars I and II.

SOUTH ATLANTIC MEDAL ASSOCIATION MEMORIAL AND THE ANTELOPE GARDEN

The South Atlantic Medal Association memorial was completed in 2012 for the 30th anniversary of the Falklands conflict. It is very similar to the memorial at the Blue Beach Cemetery in San Carlos, where some of the British casualties are buried. Flanking the main memorial tablet, there are six additional tablets which have engraved on them the cap badges of the forces that made up the Task Force that recaptured the Islands after the Argentinean Invasion in 1982.

In front of the memorial is the Antelope Garden. The garden was opened on 2 April 2007 by Captain Nick Tobin, the former Commanding Officer of HMS Antelope, which was sunk during the campaign. It is planted with Viscosa Antelope, a deciduous azalea which produces a pink fragrant flower in May.

Nearby is a tree planted by Lady Fieldhouse in memory of her husband, Admiral of the Fleet Lord Fieldhouse of Gosport, in the County of Hampshire. As Commander in Chief Fleet in 1982, John Fieldhouse was the Commander of the Task Force and given responsibility for 'Operation Corporate', the mission to recover the Falkland Islands.

APRIL - JUNE 1982

IN HONOUR OF
THE SOUTH ATLANTIC TASK FORCE
AND TO THE ABIDING MEMORY OF THE
255 SAILORS, SOLDIERS AND AIRMEN
WHO GAVE THEIR LIVES AND THOSE WHO
HAVE NO GRAVE BUT THE SEA

ROYAL NAVAL REVIEW

The collection of oak trees interspersed with memorial plinths and plaques dedicated to individual Royal Naval ships, individuals and Associations forms the Royal Naval Review. Groups remembered here include the Submariners (whose plinth shows images and details of their 14 VC holders), the Royal Naval Air Service and the Royal Marine Commandos.

The Loch Class Frigate memorial cairn is dedicated to the ships' companies who served aboard the Loch Class Frigates and their variants in World War II and all theatres up to 1970. The cairn includes stones from each of the Scottish lochs after which the Frigates were named.

HMS NEPTUNE & HMS KANDAHAR ASSOCIATION

In December 1941, HMS Kandahar together with the cruiser HMS Neptune were sunk by mines in the Mediterranean with a loss of just over 800 lives.

The second most substantial loss of life suffered by the Royal Navy in the whole of the Mediterranean campaign, the tragedy ranks among the heaviest crew losses experienced in any naval theatre of World War II.

The pyramid shaped memorial is positioned so that it aligns with the position off the coast of Libya where the wreck of HMS Neptune lies. Concealed within the stone are a roll of honour of the 837 men who died and a painting of the sky as it was on the night of the sinking. Survivors tried to swim to safety, but due to rough seas and darkness only one of the crew of 765 survived.

ARTIFICER APPRENTICES OF HMS CALEDONIA 1937 – 1985

Artificers have served in the Royal Navy since 1868. They were the men who repaired and maintained all the equipment on His or Her Majesty's ships wherever they were in the world.

Artificers have to successfully complete a four year apprenticeship and HMS Caledonia was where many Artificers were trained.

CAPTAIN CLASS FRIGATE ASSOCIATION

In 1942, the USA began to build destroyer escorts to combat German U-boat operations. 78 were leased to the Royal Navy to become 'Captain Class Frigates' (named after conspicuous naval captains). They participated in the destruction of U-boats, many E-boats and other light craft. Fifteen frigates were sunk or damaged beyond repair in action, with over 700 fatalities and many wounded.

Immediately after the War, surviving ships were returned to the USN, with the exception of HMS Hotham, retained until 1956.

HMS HOOD ASSOCIATION

The memorial commemorates the 1,415 men lost in the sinking of HMS Hood on 24 May 1941. It was dedicated on 25 October 2008.

HMS GANGES ASSOCIATION

After nearly 40 years based on the last wooden walled sea-going flag ship, HMS Ganges, the training of Boy Seamen, was transferred ashore in 1905 to Shotley, Suffolk. The establishment, which was later renamed HMS Ganges (a name that goes back 250 years), was opened as a Boy Seaman's training school, accepting boys between the ages of 15 and 16 and a half. The establishment was closed in 1976 following the raising of the school leaving age to 17 and initial training of all Naval Ratings transferred to HMS Raleigh in Cornwall. Two Boys went on to win the VC, one in World War I and the other in World War II.

HMS PRINCE OF WALES AND HMS REPULSE

HMS Prince of Wales was a King George V Class Battleship built by Cammell Laird, Birkenhead and commissioned in March 1941. She participated in the pursuit of the German battleship Bismarck and was struck seven times during the battle, resulting in the loss of 14 men. In August 1941 the Prince of Wales transported Sir Winston Churchill to meet Franklin D. Roosevelt at Placenta Bay, Newfoundland where they created the Atlantic Charter.

HMS Repulse was a Renown Class Battle Cruiser built by John Browns, Clydebank, and was commissioned in August 1916. She joined battle cruiser force as flagship No 1 Battle Cruiser Squadron and took part in the battle of Heligoland Bight. Repulse was involved in refugee work at the outbreak of the Spanish War and in 1940 operated out of Norway and on convoy duties until Summer 1941.

In December 1941 Repulse and the Prince of Wales were sunk by Japanese aircraft off Kuantan on the Malayan Coast: HMS Prince of Wales lost 327 personnel, including Admiral Sir Tom Phillips, Commander in Chief of the Eastern Fleet, and Captain John Leach, Commanding Officer of the Prince of Wales.

COASTAL FORCES VETERANS' ASSOCIATION

In 1974, the Coastal Forces Veterans' Association was formed by crews who served in the Royal Navy from 1939 to 1957 in the 'Little Ships'; Motor Torpedo Boats (MTBs), Motor Gun Boats and Motor Launches. Their motto is "To upkeep the spirit of comradeship that prevailed in the boats".

The boats took the war to the enemy, attacking ships at short range, laying and sweeping mines, defending convoys, carrying out air-sea rescue and supporting the major landings at Dunkirk, Dieppe, Sicily, Salerno and Normandy. They played a major role in the success of the St Nazaire attack, losing 14 out of 17 Motor Launches. Many decorations were awarded to officers and men, bearing witness to their gallantry and spirit.

413a

ROYAL NAVAL PATROL SERVICE

The Royal Naval Patrol Service (RNPS) was set up in August 1939. Consisting initially of 200 trawlers, drifters and whalers manned by some 6,000 fishermen, the ships were equipped with guns mostly from World War I and with anti-submarine patrol and minesweeping equipment. By the end of the war there were 66,000 men, 600 Wrens and 2,000 ships.

Minesweeping activities were vital to the task of keeping open the shipping lanes around the United Kingdom and further afield. The RNPS was involved in the Norway Campaign where Captain (then Lieutenant) Richard Stannard was awarded the Victoria Cross while in command of HMT Arab being attacked from the air at Namsos. Thousands of troops were ferried back to the UK from Dunkirk by ships of the RNPS.

As the war developed, the RNPS could be found in many naval theatres – from the eastern seaboard of the USA, where refitted trawlers were lost to the U-boats they were searching for, to the Mediterranean, where HMT Moonstone captured the Italian submarine 'Galileo Galilei'. In 1944, 235 minesweepers swept the Channel ahead of the invasion fleet.

The bravery of 'Harry Tate's Navy' or 'Churchill's pirates', as they had come to be known, is told by their losses – over 5,000 men perished, 2,385 with no known grave but the sea, and 475 ships never returned to port.

Photo by Barry Turner

DEFENSIVELY EQUIPPED MERCHANT SHIPS

In the centre of the Defensively Equipped Merchant Ships (DEMS) memorial garden is a Bofors gun of the type which were fitted on merchant ships and manned by Maritime Royal Artillery gunners.

The garden is dedicated to the impressive wartime record of the DEMS personnel. In all, 27,680 officers and ratings passed gunnery and defensive equipment courses. DEMS gunners, an integral part of the Royal Navy, were deployed on merchant ships in numbers varying from two on the smallest ships to up to 100 in the larger transporters. Sacrifices were heavy, with 2,713 gunners killed or missing. Their names can be found in a memorial book in the chapel.

MASTER MARINERS SUNDIAL

The 20 foot (six metre) diameter 'human' sundial was designed by Christopher St J H Daniel and executed in situ by Mark Frith in Dunhouse stone and blue Elterwater slate.

The dial represents an oval outline chart of the world and the shadow of a person standing on the date scale indicates Greenwich Mean Time on the surrounding numbers. So to get the correct, and very accurate, time, stand on the appropriate month, add 7 minutes (the difference in time between GMT and Alrewas) and in the summer add the extra hour.

It was presented by the Honourable Company of Master Mariners and dedicated in 2001 to commemorate the loss of 2,535 ships of the Merchant Navy and the 32,000 merchant seamen who gave their lives in World War II.

Photo by Barry Turner

Photo by OceanBarefoot

THE MERCHANT NAVY CONVOY WOOD

The Convoy is dedicated to over 46,000 British merchant seafarers and fishermen lost in conflict during the 20th Century, including two World Wars, Falklands, Kuwait, Vietnam, Iran, Iraq and others.

In World War II, 31,908 seafarers perished, proportionately more than any of the Armed Services. 2,535 trees represent the British vessels lost at that time. Their ships carried cargo, troops, armaments, ammunition and fuel to every theatre of war. They were civilians who faced the enemy and the sea with equal bravery and fortitude, to keep the supply lines open to Britain and its allies.

HMT LANCASTRIA

A simple stone memorial is located in front of the 'Lancastria Oak' within the Merchant Navy Woodland, bearing a circular plaque inscribed with the Lancastria Association badge and emblem.

On 17 June 1940, the 16,000 ton Cunard liner Lancastria lay five miles off St Nazaire embarking troops, RAF personnel and civilian refugees, including women and children, who were being evacuated from France, which was then on the point of collapse. The exact number on board may never be known, but almost certainly exceeded 6,000; some estimates were as high as 9,000. The Lancastria was attacked and hit by bombs from German aircraft. The ship sank rapidly and, according to the estimate of the Captain, only around 2,500 of those on board were saved.

Because of the scale of the tragedy, Winston Churchill forbade publication of the news, in the interests of public morale, and hence the story of the Lancastria has never been generally known, although it is Britain's worst maritime disaster.

THE MERCHANT NAVY ASSOCIATION MEMORIAL

Dedicated on the 1st October 2003, and supported by Members from 30 Branches nationally, the Memorial Stone came from a quarry in Cornwall and the white seams in the rock appear to represent the sea washing over the rocks ashore. This Memorial represents past and present Merchant Navy personnel.

416a

Photo by Barry Turner

ROYAL FLEET AUXILIARY SHIP 'SIR PERCIVALE' ANCHOR

The central glade of the Merchant Navy Convoy is an appropriate home to one of the anchors from Royal Fleet Auxiliary (RFA) Sir Percivale which has been donated by the Merchant Navy Welfare Board.

Outside the two World Wars, the largest loss of Merchant Navy lives was during the Falklands conflict. Sir Percivale landed troops in San Carlos Bay and was the first British vessel to enter Port Stanley following the Argentinian surrender. She later served in the Gulf War of 1991, was deployed in support of British operations in the Balkans and was present at the handover of Hong Kong to China. She was crewed throughout her life by officers and ratings of the Merchant Navy.

The anchor was dedicated on 8 June 2011, the anniversary of the bombing of Sir Percivale's sister ships Sir Galahad and Sir Tristram in Bluff Cove during the Falklands conflict in 1982.

Photo by Barry Turner

WOMEN'S ROYAL NAVAL SERVICE

This charming garden at the far end of the Royal Naval Review is dedicated to the Women's Royal Naval Service (WRNS).

It has been designed to encourage birds, insects and butterflies. The pathways are laid in the shape of an anchor around rose beds planted with 'Wren' roses.

Located in the garden is the Aguila Memorial, a beautifully carved wren which commemorates the 21 WRNS and one Naval Nursing Sister who were lost when SS Aguila was torpedoed in 1941. The memorial is dedicated to all who served in the Women's Royal Naval Service.

THE VOLUNTARY AID DETACHMENT (RN)

The plaque dedicated to the above is located near to the Royal Fleet Auxiliary Memorial. VAD was a voluntary organization providing field nursing services, mainly in hospitals, during World War I and World War II.

HMS BARHAM

This memorial, the adjacent bench and tree are dedicated to all crew members from the launch in October 1914 until the sinking, after being torpedoed by U-331, on the 25 November 1941.

Photo by Phil Nixon

ERECTED IN HONOUR OF
ALL WHO SAILED ON THE ARCTIC CONVOYS
1941 - 1945
THEIR GREAT SACRIFICE WAS MADE FOR OUR FREEDOM
WE WILL ALWAYS REMEMBER THEM

Монумент воздвигнут в честь всех участников Конвоев отправлявшихся из Скапа Флоу в Россию в
1941 - 1945 гг.
М всегдеа будем помнить тех,

RUSSIAN CONVOY VETERANS

June 1941 – May 1945 saw the United Kingdom help Russia by supplying them with millions of tons of war-related goods. The convoys were protected by Royal Navy ships of many types, with a loss of only 22 ships.

Men serving on these ships undertook this most hazardous journey through seas littered with floes and bergs with force 9 and 11 winds whipping the seas into mountainous waves. It was always cold, both inside and out, with the permanent duty of ice breaking from the superstructure to prevent them from capsizing and sinking. The convoys suffered constant attack from the German Navy and Air Force from their safe ports in Norway.

Churchill called it "The worst journey in the world".

417a

ARMY DOG UNIT (NORTHERN IRELAND) ASSOCIATION RED PAW

This memorial was dedicated on 1st August 2009 to the memory of those, both humans and animals, who lost their lives whilst serving in the Army Dog Unit, Northern Ireland.

It is made from polished black granite designed in a wedge shape with an engraved face. The PAW graphics and words "Search and Secure" are the Association's motto.

Photo by Barry Turner

417b

Photo by Phil Nixon

REMEMBERING THE NAVAL NURSING

THE QUEEN ALEXANDRA'S ROYAL NAVAL NURSING SERVICE AND THE VOLUNTARY AID DETACHMENT (RN)

At the corner of the Merchant Navy Convoy and the Ulster Ash Grove, a blue pearl granite tablet is dedicated to all who served, and continue to serve, in The Queen Alexandra's Royal Naval Nursing Service (QARNNS) and the Voluntary Aid Detachment (RN).

Matching curved benches are flanked each side by a rowan tree, known as the 'healing' tree. Its berries are used for medical purposes and its wood was used to make handles for stretchers during World War I.

418

Photo by Barry Turner

418a

Photo by Phil Nixon

ULSTER SPECIAL CONSTABULARY

The black marble and blue limestone monument was dedicated on 29 July 2006 as a tribute to 50 years of public-spirited service on the part of the Ulster Special Constabulary.

Formed in October 1920 by Sir Ernest Clark, Additional Assistant Under-secretary in the Irish Office, the new Special Constabulary comprised three categories. Firstly, the 'A' Specials who were paid and worked full-time with the same arms and equipment as the Royal Ulster Constabulary; secondly, the 'B' Specials who were part-time and unpaid apart from a small allowance for clothing and whose arms were determined by the police county commander; and thirdly, the 'C' Specials, a reserve force called out in emergencies. By the end of 1920, the Ulster Special Constabulary totalled 3,500 'A', 16,000 'B' and over 1,000 'C' Constables. The Ulster Special Constabulary was stood down on 30 April 1970.

THE ROYAL BRITISH LEGION NEVER FORGET TRIBUTE GARDEN

The Never Forget Tribute Garden is a unique and personal memorial where a sponsor chooses the date on which they want to remember a loved one and an everlasting poppy is dedicated to that person's memory. The Poppy, bearing the name of the person being remembered, is then planted in the bed for the month in which their relatives and friends wish to remember them.

ARMED SERVICES WOOD

A woodland of mixed trees individually sponsored as living tributes to those who served in the British Army, the Royal Navy and the Royal Air Force.

LIONS CLUB INTERNATIONAL – WOODEN SHELTER

This shelter is dedicated to the memory of Lions from Great Britain and Ireland in grateful thanks for their service.

The Lions is a charitable organisation dedicated to serving local, national and international communities.

Photo by Barry Turner

DOUGLAS SKENE GROVE

Douglas Skene (1948 – 2007) was a dedicated military historian, a serving officer in the Royal Scots Greys and a member of the Territorial Army with the Royal Green Jackets. He practiced as an independent financial consultant but his hobby was to lead tours to World War I battlefields. His other great love was trees and he enjoyed watching the Arboretum develop from its inception until his untimely death at the age of 59. Following his death, his family, friends and colleagues raised funds towards setting up the first grove of specimen trees at the Arboretum, a lasting legacy to his memory.

Trees in the Grove include **Berberis valdiviana**, the barberry from Chile; **Aesculus flava**, the sweet buckeye from South-East USA; **Cupressus funebris**, the Chinese weeping cypress from central China; and **Pinus parviflora**, the Japanese white pine.

Photo by Barry Turner

THE ULSTER ASH GROVE

The Ulster Ash Grove has been planted as a living tribute to the members of the Royal Ulster Constabulary GC, the Royal Ulster Constabulary Reserve, the Armed Forces and other organisations in the service of the crown, who lost their lives during the troubles in Northern Ireland between 1969 and 2001.

The weeping ash trees planted within the grove represent lives lost in the cause of peace in Northern Ireland and form an ever-changing backdrop to the stone circle and Mourne granite pillar. The circle contains one block of stone quarried from each of the six counties and are placed to form a symbolic map of Northern Ireland. The Ulster Grove memorial was dedicated on 23 September 2003, the anniversary of the death of the first soldier in 1969.

THE ULSTER DEFENCE REGIMENT CGC

In proud remembrance of all the men and women of the UDR who gave their lives 1970 – 1992.

CGC stands for Conspicuous Gallantry Cross.

Photo by Phil Nixon

THE
ULSTER
DEFENCE
REGIMENT
CGC
1970-1992
IN
PROUD
REMEMBRANCE
OF ALL THE
MEN AND WOMEN
OF THE
ULSTER
DEFENCE
REGIMENT
WHO GAVE
THEIR LIVES

AS POPPY PETALS GENTLY FALL
REMEMBER US WHO GAVE OUR ALL

Photo by Phil Nixon

THE RUC GC WAY

The Royal Ulster Constabulary GC Way was designed in memory of the Royal Ulster Constabulary police officers who lost their lives whilst protecting life and property, preventing and detecting crime and keeping the community safe in Northern Ireland from 1922 – 2001.

The Juniper trees lining the Way represent the 38 Sub-Divisional policing areas of the Province in which the officers worked and were killed or injured while carrying out their duties.

The Mourne Black Granite Stone, in the centre of the way, with the RUC and George Cross crests inscribed, acknowledges the outstanding dedication and commitment these officers gave whilst upholding law and order in Northern Ireland.

THE HOME FRONT

Home Front is the informal term commonly used to describe the civilian populace of the nation at war as an active support system of its military. The large quarried stone with a memorial plaque was dedicated on 20 May 2006 as a tribute to those who worked on the home front to support the war effort from 1939 to 1945. The people of Burton-on-Trent, including the Fire Service, donated the memorial.

THE NATIONAL EX-PRISONER OF WAR ASSOCIATION

A memorial dedicated to the memory of those who fell by the wayside on the many routes from Polish POW camps was built in Fallingbostel, Germany, by members of 2 Battn REME.

Veterans of those journeys marched in appalling conditions. Many suffered diseases such as typhoid and diphtheria or carried wounds inflicted prior to or after capture. All were malnourished and had inadequate clothing and equipment to protect them during one of Germany's worst recorded winters. The memorial here was also built by members of 2 Battn REME and Royal Engineers and is an exact replica of the one in Fallingbostel. It is dedicated to the memory of those made prisoner in World War II theatres in Scandinavia, Europe, the Middle East and North Africa.

Photo by Barry Turner

National Memorial Arboretum

422

Map reference

THE CHILDREN'S WOODLAND / ACTIVITY AREA

Sponsored by the Midlands Co-operative Society Limited and planted with over a 1,000 native British trees, the Children's Woodland was designed to combine arboriculture and wildlife education with Remembrance.

Individual trees have been sponsored by families and schools and dedicated to babies and children who have passed away. In the nearby shelter are large child-sized wooden figures of the characters from 'The Wind in the Willows' by Kenneth Grahame, carved by the Essex Woodcarvers under the supervision of Peter Benson, Chairman of the Master Woodcarvers' Association.

The Arboretum children's activity area and picnic area was funded by Staffordshire Aggregates Levy Grant Scheme (SALGS). It is a purpose-built wooden environment for children aged between 7 – 13 years.

Photo by Barry Turner

THE EDWARD'S TRUST GARDEN

The Edward's Trust is a charity that provides bereavement services to children and families.

Designed by Hannah Genders, The Edward's Trust Garden aims to immediately connect people with the garden and its purpose. The design of the tree, sculpted by David Watkinson, and surrounding area pays attention to the grief experience. Fundamental to this are the symbols of 'hope' and the importance of care and support to those who grieve.

The garden has won two British Association of Landscape Industries (BALI) Awards – landscape design excellence award and a special award for innovative design.

FELLOWSHIP OF THE SERVICES

In this peaceful setting alongside the River Tame, 114 trees have been planted as a living tribute to the Fellowship of the Services and to keep alive the memory of the individual Messes who have sponsored the grove.

A Brotherhood of officers and men, Fellowship is the underlying spirit of comradeship proved in the fires of two World Wars and perpetuated in a 'Brotherhood' of ex-servicemen drawn from all ranks of HM Forces. The majority are officers and men who served in these wars and carry on a Service Brotherhood, an association created out of the unforgettable experiences of World War I.

Photo by Phil Nixon

MILLENNIUM WOOD

A woodland of individually sponsored mixed variety trees with remembrance plaques and labels.

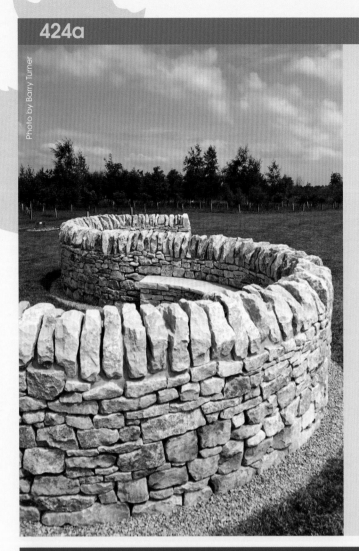

Photo by Barry Turner

WOMEN'S INSTITUTE

The Women's Institute (WI) dry stone wall with seats was designed and built by Derbyshire's only registered female dry stonewaller, Sally Hodgson. The stone was donated by Longcliffe Quarry, Brassington.

The curving wall includes seats facing in two directions, one side looking out at the River Tame and the other along the beautiful meadow planted with poppies and wild flowers.

The dedication, on 22 June 2009, was attended by the Dowager Duchess of Devonshire, a past Patron of the National Dry Stone Walling Association and a member of the WI for over 75 years.

THE SALVATION ARMY

General William Booth founded 'The Christian Mission' in 1865. The organisation was renamed 'The Salvation Army' in 1878. Members came from all walks of life and were to be found in both the Royal Navy and the regular Army.

The Salvation Army operates in 126 countries, offering practical support, unconditional friendship and practical help to people of all ages, backgrounds and needs. Being a Salvationist was, and is, no easy option. Bravery in the service of God had its parallels in service to the King and country.

The memorial, located at the bottom of the Poppy Field, was designed by Mel Gilman. It is made of toughened glass and is engraved with two outstretched hands and the inscription "Be still and know that I am God" from Psalm 46:10.

YMCA

In remembrance of all those who, through the YMCA, served the armed forces in times of war and peace, some of whom gave their lives in the service of others. The YMCA is an international Christian movement helping people to develop in mind, body and spirit, supporting families and strengthening communities, welcoming those of all faiths and those of none.

Photo by Phil Nixon

COMBINED OPERATIONS COMMAND MEMORIAL

Combined Operations were the Army, Navy and Air Forces working together as a unified force under a single command, the motto of which was, appropriately, 'United we Conquer'.

When Churchill set up the combined Operations Command in the summer of 1940, an invasion of the UK seemed imminent. The Command was immediately tasked to harass the enemy along the coasts of occupied countries with friendly populations. To accomplish these tasks, Combined Operations set up a vast training programme, culminating in joint exercises in amphibious landing techniques. As preparations for war progressed, the service personnel of many Allied Nations served in, or alongside, Combined Operations. The Command also oversaw work on the Mulberry Harbours, the PLUTO Fuel pipelines and Hobart's tank adaptations for beach clearance work, all of which were part of the offensive operations Churchill bestowed on the Command.

425

Photo by Barry Turner

THE ROYAL BRITISH LEGION POPPY FIELD

The Royal British Legion is a leading Service and ex-Service organisation and one of the UK's most established and respected charities. Its principal concern is the welfare of ex-Service personnel and their dependants, with around 11 million people in the UK eligible for that support.

The Royal British Legion Avenue is a 200m grove lined with 44 5m tall English oaks. Poppy seeds have been sown between the oaks to initiate the Poppy Field which will gradually become self-seeding and will create a stunning feature in May and June each year. As they grow, the avenue of oaks will become a dramatic feature, giving a tree-lined vista across the site when viewed from next to the wartime pillbox on the bank of the River Tame.

425a

THE SPIRITUALISTS' NATIONAL UNION

The memorial was dedicated on Saturday 10 July 2010 in memory of Spiritualists who have served and continue to serve in the British and Commonwealth Armed Forces, and all Spiritualists who have served their country in times of conflict.

The memorial comprises a circular bench made from polished beige granite topped with curved coping slabs to form a seat. Within the bench are seven curved pieces of Balmoral red granite, each one bearing symbolic words.

The internal floor of the circle is paved with the same two types of granite, depicting a seven pointed star. Standing in the centre of the circle is an obelisk with a pyramid top.

Photo by Phil Nixon

QUAKER SERVICES MEMORIAL

During both World Wars, members of the Religious Society of Friends (Quakers) were active in relief work, which was recognised by the award of the Nobel Peace Prize in 1947. The citation covered humanitarian service since the Irish famine a century earlier.

The Friends Ambulance Unit was an independent body led by Quakers and open to people of all denominations, giving conscientious objectors to military service an opportunity to serve in theatres of war. Bronze stars set in the paving mark the seventeen lives lost.

The Friends Relief Service was the official arm of the Society for the relief of civilian distress. Twelve hundred people, nearly half of them women, from all denominations served as members.

The circular design of the memorial, which symbolises reconciliation between opponents, invites visitors to rest and contemplate; it also represents the unity and equality which Friends bring to their worship and lives. Quakers recognise the reality of conflict, and have practical experience of the power of love in its resolution.

Photo by Barry Turner

RAC FUTURE FORESTS

Future Forests is a scheme that measures emissions of carbon dioxide, the greenhouse gas which scientists think is responsible for global warming. The scheme helps to offset this pollution by planting natural forests and woodlands and investing in renewable energy.

The Royal Automobile Club (RAC) Future Forests wood was sponsored by the RAC as part of the Future Forests scheme and as a tribute to their employees who have now retired.

THE ROADPEACE WOOD

The memorial has been designed to represent a circular tarmac traffic island with the RoadPeace insignia of a dove and a memorial plaque in the centre.

The memorial with its individually sponsored trees and benches is in memory of victims of road accidents and has been sponsored by RoadPeace, a charity that supports people who have suffered bereavement or injury through road accidents.

Photo by Barry Turner

Photo by Phil Nixon

ALLIED SPECIAL FORCES ASSOCIATION GROVE

The Allied Special Forces Association Grove is a living memorial, in harmony with nature and growing in stature. It is a place for remembrance, commemoration, education and quiet contemplation. It is being laid out in the form of an "Open Air Book", where you can read about individuals and military units who served with Allied Special Forces during World War II and up to the present day.

The Grove has a Sun Room shelter at its heart, with fine views down each avenue. It is reached by a disabled / wheelchair friendly memorial way, which gently meanders past the memorials, trees and shrubs and is maintained financially by members of the association and their friends in support of the National Memorial Arboretum and its "Spirit of Remembrance".

The Grove is sub-divided into seven garden areas:

• Special Operations
• Friends of our association
• Raids, Raiders and Resistance Forces
• Soldiers of 22 SAS
• Commandos
• Falkland Islands Resistance
• Airborne Forces

and contains 45 memorials; 134 individuals and 84 military units are named here.

The Grove is set beside the River Tame and quarry lakes and is reached by a road along the river bank.

WESTERN FRONT ASSOCIATION MEMORIAL

The Western Front Association (WFA) is an historical interest group established in 1980 by noted military historian John Giles and has a worldwide membership of over 6,500. The WFA supports many remembrance and research projects, including the renovation of battlefield memorials.

Hornbeams propagated from the only tree in Delville Wood to survive the Battle of the Somme have been planted, and most are individually dedicated.

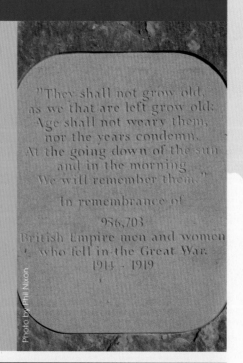

"They shall not grow old,
as we that are left grow old:
Age shall not weary them,
nor the years condemn.
At the going down of the sun
and in the morning
We will remember them."

In remembrance of

956,703

British Empire men and women
who fell in the Great War.
1914 – 1919

Photo by Phil Nixon

Photo by Phil Nixon

UNITED NATIONS AVENUE

This is an avenue of giant redwoods planted alongside the mainline railway bridge, which will be clearly visible from passing trains as the trees grow.

Member countries of the United Nations have sponsored the trees and plaques.

THE FORESTERS FRIENDLY SOCIETY

The industrial revolution caused mass movement of workers from the land to the mills of Northern England. The Ancient Order of Foresters Friendly Society was formed in 1834 to provide fraternal mutual support to members in times of sickness and bereavement. These aims continue.

Two members were decorated for valour in the 1914 – 1918 conflict:

- Bro I / Cpl W. Fuller VC, 2nd Welsh Regiment. Court 5360
- Bro I / Cpl W. Angus VC, 8th Lanark Bn, Highland Light Infantry. Court 6416

431

WATERSMEET

Watersmeet is a native British riverside wood comprising silver birch, black poplar and willow between the railway bridge and the confluence of the rivers Tame and Trent. The woodland was planted with the assistance of the International Tree Foundation's Family Tree Scheme and encompasses both Lovejoy Wood and Mac's Wood which celebrate the lives of Professor Derek Lovejoy and Meg Carroll respectively.

Nearby is the Mythaholme Footbridge. The bridge was installed by the Central Rivers Initiative, a partnership to ensure the successful regeneration of this section of the Trent and Tame valleys after quarrying. Mythaholme is an Old English word meaning 'the space between the merging of two rivers'.

Photo by David McDonnell

DURING THE CURRENT REDEVELOPMENT BUILDING PROJECT, A NUMBER OF MEMORIALS ARE BEING RETAINED IN STORAGE AND WILL BE REINSTATED IN NEW LOCATIONS.

THESE INCLUDE THE FOLLOWING:

SSAFA

SSAFA provides lifelong support to anyone who is currently serving or has ever served in the Royal Navy, British Army or Royal Air Force. The charity was founded in 1885 and has been here for our Forces and their families for more than 125 years, helping millions of people in that time. SSAFA's regional network of trained volunteers throughout the UK and on military bases around the world means that support is always close at hand.

The memorial shows the SSAFA crest.

THE BRITISH BERLIN AIRLIFT MONUMENT

This memorial and grove are in tribute to those who took part in the Berlin Airlift, the operation to deliver food and supplies to a besieged Berlin, between June 1948 and May 1949.

The memorial plinth, created by the sculptor Andy de Comyn, is curved and has three ribs as a symbol of the three air lanes into Berlin from the French, British and American sectors of West Berlin. Members of the Essex Woodcarvers carved the life sized Golden Eagle which is coming in to land on top. The wood used is Iroko. The avenue of 39 fruit trees behind the plinth is planted to commemorate the lives of the 39 personnel lost during the airlift.

The feasibility of supplying two million Berliners by air alone was first proposed by RAF Air Commodore Rex Waite. As a result 2.326m tons of supplies were airlifted into Berlin. 31% was flown in on British aircraft in 175,000 flights involving over 30 million miles of flying.

CADET FORCES' GARDEN

The circular seat with surrounding planting was sponsored by the Army Cadet Force, a national voluntary youth organization for young people aged 12 – 18, to honour former members of the Cadet Forces who went on to join the Armed Forces and subsequently lost their lives.

The garden uses plant species that grow in drier conditions such as senecios, phormiums and euphorbias. This is a particularly sunny area for visitors to sit and rest.

In 2010, the Cadet Force's 150th anniversary year, a rededication service was held and a plaque placed in the paving was unveiled.

AMBULANCE SERVICES

This garden was dedicated on 16 September 2004 and designed in the shape of an A – not only the initial letter of the service, but also to stand for 'Asclepius', the Greek God of healing and medicine.

There are six prehistoric Dawn redwood trees to the right of the garden, and three rowan trees to the left. The significance of the rowan is that it was used to make the handles of stretchers in World War I. Other shrubs you will see around the garden are Skimmia japonica, Berberis darwinnii and dogwood, all used historically for healing.

The memorial garden has been created as a lasting tribute to all ambulance personnel who have died, but especially to those who have been killed on duty 'in service' to others.

SUPPORTING THE ARBORETUM

As a charity, the Arboretum relies on the generous support of individuals and organisations to maintain this unique and special free-entry site of national significance.

Help us continue to grow and improve the Arboretum, enabling more families and colleagues to remember the sacrifice of loved ones in this spiritually uplifting place. We are grateful for all gifts, large or small, which make it possible to continue our vital work.

DONATIONS

SINGLE GIFT

If you would like to make a single donation there are a number of ways to do this…

Cash
Make a cash donation at one of our donation boxes in the Visitor Centre today.

Online
To make a single donation on our website, please visit: www.thenma.org.uk.

Card
You can make a donation by debit or credit card in our shop or kiosk, as well as over the phone, call us on 01283 792 333.

Cheque
If you would like to support us by sending a cheque our address is: National Memorial Arboretum, Croxall Road, Alrewas, Staffordshire DE13 7AR.

REGULAR GIVING

You may wish to support us with a regular donation, either monthly, annually or biannually. To set up a regular donation by direct debit, simply visit our website: www.thenma.org.uk. Alternatively, please speak to a member of our team to find out how you can set up a standing order.

FUNDRAISING PACK
Help keep the memories alive at the
National Memorial Arboretum

Plan your visit www.thenma.org.uk

NATIONAL MEMORIAL ARBORETUM FRIENDS

Become a Friend today and support the Arboretum with a regular gift, either monthly or annually, whilst benefitting from a quarterly newsletter and increased involvement with the Arboretum. You can find out more information about becoming a Friend, and also download a membership application form, on our website, alternatively call us on 01283 792 333 or email **friends@thenma.org.uk**.

LEAVE A GIFT IN YOUR WILL

Making a gift in your will means your generous support and commitment to Remembrance can continue long after your lifetime.

To find out more about supporting the National Memorial Arboretum in your will, you can collect a legacy information pack from a member of our team. Alternatively, you can request a legacy pack by calling us on: 01283 792 333 or by emailing **info@thenma.org.uk**.

FUNDRAISE FOR US

There are many ways to raise money for the Arboretum. Our fundraising pack is full of great ideas and advice to get you started. To receive our fundraising pack, call us on 01283 792 333 or visit our website... Don't forget to create your own Just Giving page or visit our page **www.justgiving/thenma** to collect online donations.

GIFT AID IT

Please don't forget to make your gift worth 25% more, at no extra cost to you!

If you are a UK tax payer, and pay an amount of Income Tax and / or Capital Gains Tax at least equal to the tax the charity reclaims on your behalf, the National Memorial Arboretum can increase the value of your donation by 25%. Thank you for your support.

DONATION FORM AND INFORMATION

YOUR CONTACT DETAILS:

Title:........................ Surname:...

Forenames:...

Address:..

....

....

Postcode:..

Telephone:..

Email:..

PLEASE LET US KNOW WHAT INFORMATION YOU WOULD LIKE TO RECEIVE

Leaflets and forms for
(please tick the items you would like to receive):

Joining the Friends ☐

Group Booking or Events ☐

Leaving a Legacy ☐

Making a Donation ☐

Fundraising or Sponsorship ☐

Volunteering ☐

DONATION (OPTIONAL):

I enclose a donation of £...
Please make cheques payable to the
National Memorial Arboretum and sign the Gift Aid declaration if you are able to.

WHAT SHOULD I DO WITH THIS FORM?

Once you have filled out all the details simply cut free of the guide book, or photocopy the page, and either:

1. Hand it to one of our members of staff on Reception, or

2. Place it in an envelope and post to us at: National Memorial Arboretum, Croxall Road, Alrewas, Staffordshire, DE13 7AR

DONATE ONLINE:

Alternatively you could donate online at http://www.thenma.org.uk/get-involved/donation/

GIFT AID DECLARATION

giftaid it

Gift Aid (paid to us by the Government) increases a donation of £100 to £125*

Declaration: "I wish you to treat as Gift Aid all donations that I make to the National Memorial Arboretum, Charity No. 1043992, from now until I notify otherwise. I understand that my donations are eligible to be treated as Gift Aid if I pay an amount of UK Income Tax or Capital Gains Tax at least equal to my Gift Aid donations in the tax year."

Signed...

Date ....

*Accurate at time of print.

THANK YOU!

**We need
nearly £4,000**
every day to ensure
the Arboretum is
free to enter

ALPHABETICAL
MEMORIAL INDEX

Memorial	Pg	No
1ST AIRBORNE RECONNAISSANCE SQUADRON	34	212b
1ST ARMY	77	313
8TH ARMY AND TOBRUK	77	313
9/12 LANCERS	73	309
10TH ROYAL HUSSARS	76	311b
11TH ROYAL HUSSARS (THE CHERRY PICKERS)	76	311b
17/21 LANCERS	73	309
17TH DOGRA REGIMENT	59	236
THE 41 CLUB	110	338
90 SIGNALS UNIT	120	346a
1940 DUNKIRK VETERANS' ASSOCIATION	21	101
II (ARMY COOPERATION) SQUADRON	112	340
ADJUTANT GENERAL'S CORPS COMMEMORATIVE GARDEN	120	348
AIRCREW ASSOCIATION MEMORIAL	117	343a
AIR FORMATION AND AIR SUPPORT SIGNALS	119	346
ALLIED SPECIAL FORCES ASSOCIATION GROVE	162	428
AMBULANCE SERVICES	166	IN STORAGE
ANCIENT BURIAL MOUND	111	339
ANGLO-JAPANESE PEACE GARDEN	84	319
ARMED FORCES MEMORIAL ©️	9	–
ARMED SERVICES WOOD	151	419
ARMY AIR CORPS	80	313b
ARMY APPRENTICE NATIONAL MEMORIAL	99	331a
THE ARMY BENEVOLENT FUND – THE SOLDIERS' CHARITY	29	205
ARMY DOG UNIT (NORTHERN IRELAND) ASSOCIATION RED PAW	149	417a
THE ARMY PARADE	75	311
THE ARMY WOOD	80	313a
ASSOCIATION OF JEWISH EX-SERVICEMEN AND WOMEN	121	350

Memorial	Pg	No
AUXILIARY TERRITORIAL SERVICE / ACK ACK	40	220
AUXILIARY TERRITORIAL SERVICE STATUE	31	208
BALUCH REGIMENT	62	241
BASRA MEMORIAL WALL	85	321a
THE BEAT (POLICE MEMORIAL AVENUE)	69	305
THE BEVIN BOYS MEMORIAL	33	211
BIDADARI CEMETERY	131	403
BIRMINGHAM CHILDREN'S HOSPITAL	99	331
BLESMA EXTENSION	131	404
THE BLIND VETERANS UK (ST DUNSTAN'S) PATHWAY	28	202
THE BLUES AND ROYALS	86	323
THE BOYS' BRIGADE	30	206a
BRIGADE OF GURKHAS	60	236
THE BRITISH BERLIN AIRLIFT MONUMENT	165	IN STORAGE
BRITISH GERMAN FRIENDSHIP GARDEN	83	318
BRITISH LIMBLESS EX-SERVICE MEN'S ASSOCIATION (BLESMA)	38	217
BRITISH KOREAN VETERANS ASSOCIATION	59	235
BRITISH NUCLEAR TEST VETERANS	136	411
BRITISH SOUTH AFRICA POLICE	129	401a
BROTHERHOOD OF GREEK VETERANS CHAPEL	72	308
BURMA RAILWAY	53	230
BURMA STAR	57	232
CADET FORCES' GARDEN	166	IN STORAGE
CAVALRY GROVE (CRESCENT)	73	309
CELEBRATION OF LIFE GROVE	84	320
CHANGI LYCH GATE	47	227
THE CHELTENHAM COLLEGE MEMORIAL	107	336
THE CHILDREN'S WOODLAND / 🅕 ACTIVITY AREA	155	422
THE CHINDIT MEMORIAL	58	232a
WOMEN'S AUXILIARY SERVICE – THE CHINTHE WOMEN	54	231
CHURCH LADS' & CHURCH GIRLS' BRIGADE	29	206
CIVIL DEFENCE	45	225

ALPHABETICAL
MEMORIAL INDEX

Memorial	Pg	No
THE CLOISTERS (B)	27	–
COMBINED OPERATIONS COMMAND MEMORIAL	158	424a
THE COMMANDOS	137	411a
COASTAL COMMAND	105	336
COMMANDER DAVID CHILDS' TREES	87	327
DEFENSIVELY EQUIPPED MERCHANT SHIPS	144	414
DIAMOND GROVE	133	408
DOUGLAS SKENE GROVE	151	419a
THE DUKE OF WELLINGTONS' REGIMENT	75	311c
THE DURHAM LIGHT INFANTRY	102	332
THE EDWARD'S TRUST GARDEN	156	422a
THE EX-NATIONAL SERVICEMEN'S MEMORIAL	30	207
FAR EAST AIR FORCE	133	407
THE FAR EAST PRISONERS OF WAR MEMORIAL BUILDING (G)	48	–
THE FAR EAST PRISONERS OF WAR GROVE	51	229
THE FAULD EXPLOSION MEMORIAL	37	214
FELLOWSHIP OF THE SERVICES	156	423
FIRE AND RESCUE SERVICES	43	223
FLEET AIR ARM	135	410
THE FORESTERS FRIENDLY SOCIETY	163	430
THE FREEMASONS	68	304
GALLIPOLI	122	351
GARDEN OF THE INNOCENTS	79	313
GCHQ MEMORIAL	98	331
GENERAL POST OFFICE MEMORIAL GARDEN	36	213
GEORGE CROSS ISLAND ASSOCIATION (MALTA)	77	313

Memorial	Pg	No
GIRLS VENTURE CORPS	107	336
GLIDER PILOT REGIMENT	35	212c
THE GOLDEN GROVE	88	327
THE GREEN HOWARDS	75	311c
HMS BARHAM	148	417
THE HOME FRONT	153	421
THE HONG KONG VOLUNTEER DEFENCE CORPS	55	231
HOME SERVICE FORCE	123	353
HOUSEHOLD DIVISION	100	332
THE INNER WHEEL GROVE	39	219
THE INTELLIGENCE CORPS	98	331
INTERNATIONAL MILITARY MUSIC SOCIETY	28	204
IRAQ / AFGHANISTAN WILLOWS	84	321
IRISH INFANTRY GROVE	87	326
ITALY STAR ASSOCIATION 1943 – 1945	77	313
KENYA POLICE	82	315
KING'S AFRICAN RIFLES	67	302
KINGFISHER WOOD	98	331
THE LEONARD CHESHIRE AMPHITHEATRE	32	210
LICHFIELD & DISTRICT GARDEN	32	209
LICHFIELD WOOD	95	330
LIGHT INFANTRY MEMORIAL	101	332
LIONS CLUB INTERNATIONAL – WOODEN SHELTER	151	419
MALAYA AND BORNEO VETERANS MEMORIAL	60	237
MALAYAN VOLUNTEER FORCE	61	239
THE MALL	102	332
MASTER MARINERS SUNDIAL	144	415

ALPHABETICAL MEMORIAL INDEX

Memorial	Pg	No
MEDITERRANEAN CAMPAIGNS OF WORLD WAR II	77	313
MEMORIAL FOR ST JOHN VOLUNTEERS	131	403a
THE MERCHANT NAVY ASSOCIATION MEMORIAL	146	416
THE MERCHANT NAVY CONVOY WOOD	145	416
MERCIAN VOLUNTEERS	123	352
MERCIAN WOOD	86	325
THE MILLENNIUM CHAPEL OF PEACE AND FORGIVENESS (B)	13	–
MILLENNIUM WOOD	156	424
THE MONTE CASSINO ASSOCIATION MEMORIAL	77	313
NATIONAL ASSOCIATION OF MEMORIAL MASONS	134	409a
THE NATIONAL EX-PRISONER OF WAR ASSOCIATION	154	421a
THE NAVY WOOD	85	322
NO 30 SQUADRON ASSOCIATION	115	341a
NORMANDY VETERANS	67	301
NORTHERN RHODESIA POLICE MEMORIAL	130	402a
NORWEGIAN NAVY FLAGPOLES	22	107a
NYASALAND POLICE MEMORIAL	130	401b
OPERATION MARKET GARDEN / MARKET GARDEN VETERANS' ASSOCIATION	34	212a
PALESTINE VETERANS' ASSOCIATION	77	313
THE PALESTINE POLICE OLD COMRADES' ASSOCIATION	77	313
THE PARACHUTE REGIMENT AND AIRBORNE FORCES	103	332
THE PHANTOM MEMORIAL	73	310
THE POLAR BEAR MEMORIAL	71	307

Memorial	Pg	No
POLICE MEMORIAL GARDEN	70	306
POLISH FORCES WAR MEMORIAL (E)	89	327a
THE PRINCE OF WALES OWN REGIMENT OF YORKSHIRE	75	311c
PRINCESS MARY'S RAF NURSING SERVICE	118	344
QUAKER SERVICES MEMORIAL	160	425b
THE QUEEN ALEXANDRA'S ROYAL ARMY NURSING CORPS	88	327
THE QUEEN ALEXANDRA'S ROYAL NAVAL NURSING SERVICE AND THE VOLUNTARY AID DETACHMENT (RN)	149	417b
1ST THE QUEEN'S DRAGOON GUARDS	102	332
THE QUEEN'S ROYAL HUSSARS	73	309
THE QUEEN'S ROYAL LANCERS	73	309
RAC FUTURE FORESTS	161	426
RAF NO. 31 SQUADRON MEMORIAL	118	344
RAF 214 SQUADRON	118	344
RAF ADMINISTRATIVE APPRENTICES	107	336
RAF AIR LOADMASTERS' ASSOCIATION	118	344
RAF AIR FORMATION SQUADRON CRESCENT	118	344
RAF BENEVOLENT FUND	112	340
RAF LOCKING	106	336
RAF MEDICAL SERVICES	118	344
RAF SEARCH & RESCUE	118	344
THE RAIL INDUSTRY	106	336
THE RECONCILIATION STONE	84	319
THE ROADPEACE WOOD	161	427
THE ROTARY RIDGE	58	234
ROYAL AIR FORCES ASSOCIATION REMEMBRANCE GARDEN	113	340a
ROYAL AIR FORCE BOY ENTRANTS	105	335
ROYAL AIR FORCE CRANWELL APPRENTICES	105	334

ALPHABETICAL
MEMORIAL INDEX

Memorial	Pg	No
ROYAL AIR FORCE HALTON APPRENTICES MEMORIAL GARDEN	37	215
THE ROYAL AIR FORCE POLICE	118	344a
ROYAL AIR FORCE REGIMENT	43	222
ROYAL AIR FORCE SERVICING COMMANDO AND TACTICAL SUPPLY WING ASSOCIATION	116	342
ROYAL AIR FORCE WING	118	344
ROYAL AIR FORCE WOOD	104	333
ROYAL ARMY DENTAL CORPS	92	328
ROYAL ARMY MEDICAL CORPS	91	328
THE ROYAL ARTILLERY GARDEN	39	218
ROYAL AUSTRALIAN AIR FORCE	120	347
ROYAL AUXILIARY AIR FORCE	116	343
THE ROYAL BRITISH LEGION NEVER FORGET TRIBUTE GARDEN	150	418a
THE ROYAL BRITISH LEGION POPPY FIELD	159	425
ROYAL CANADIAN AIR FORCE	117	344
ROYAL CORPS OF SIGNALS	87	325a
ROYAL ELECTRICAL AND MECHANICAL ENGINEERS (REME)	104	332
THE ROYAL ENGINEERS	68	303
ROYAL FLEET AUXILIARY SHIP 'SIR PERCIVALE' ANCHOR	146	416a
THE ROYAL DRAGOON GUARDS	73	309
ROYAL GLOUCESTERSHIRE, BERKSHIRE AND WILTSHIRE REGIMENT	96	330
THE ROYAL GREEN JACKETS	75	311a
THE ROYAL HAMPSHIRE REGIMENT	78	313
ROYAL HONG KONG POLICE	130	402
ROYAL INDIAN NAVY AND INDIAN ARMY	133	406
ROYAL LOGISTIC CORPS	81	314
ROYAL MALAYSIA POLICE	61	238
ROYAL MARINES ASSOCIATION	136	410a

Memorial	Pg	No
ROYAL MILITARY POLICE ASSOCIATION	82	316
ROYAL NATIONAL LIFEBOAT INSTITUTION	108	337
ROYAL NAVAL PATROL SERVICE	143	413a
ROYAL NAVAL REVIEW	141	413
ROYAL NORFOLK REGIMENT, SUFFOLK REGIMENT AND CAMBRIDGESHIRE REGIMENT MEMORIAL	56	231a
ROYAL NORWEGIAN NAVY	134	409
THE ROYAL OBSERVER CORPS	111	340
ROYAL & SUN ALLIANCE MEMORIALS	115	341
ROYAL TANK REGIMENT	86	324
THE RUC GC WAY	153	420a
RUSSIAN CONVOY VETERANS	148	417
THE SALVATION ARMY	157	424a
SECOND TACTICAL AIR FORCE MEMORIAL	118	344
SHACKLETON ASSOCIATION MEMORIAL	109	337a
SHOT AT DAWN (D)	93	329
THE SHOWMEN'S GUILD OF GREAT BRITAIN	97	330a
THE SHRIEVALTY AVENUE	122	350a
SHROPSHIRE YEOMANRY MEMORIAL PLINTH	138	411b
SSAFA	165	IN STORAGE
SOROPTIMIST INTERNATIONAL	83	317
SOUTH ATLANTIC MEDAL ASSOCIATION MEMORIAL AND THE ANTELOPE GARDEN	139	412
SPECIAL CONSTABULARY	70	305
THE SPIRITUALISTS' NATIONAL UNION	159	425a
STAFFORDSHIRE REGIMENT	121	349
STAFFORDSHIRE YEOMANRY	138	411b
STILLBIRTH AND NEONATAL DEATH CHARITY MEMORIAL (SANDS)	41	221
SUEZ VETERANS ASSOCIATION'	46	226

ALPHABETICAL MEMORIAL INDEX

Memorial	Pg	No
SULTAN OF OMAN'S ARMED FORCES MEMORIAL	62	240
THE SUMATRA RAILWAY	49	228
TOBRUK	77	313
TOC H	124	354
THE TREFOIL GUILD WILLOW SCULPTURES	38	216
TWIN TOWERS MEMORIAL	44	223
THE ULSTER ASH GROVE	152	420
ULSTER SPECIAL CONSTABULARY	150	418
THE ULSTER DEFENCE REGIMENT CGC	152	420
UNITED NATIONS AVENUE	163	430
THE VOLUNTARY AID DETACHMENT (RN)	148	417
THE WAR WIDOWS' ROSE GARDEN	79	313
WAR WIDOWS' WOOD AND MEMORIAL	76	312
WATERSMEET	164	431
WESTERN FRONT ASSOCIATION MEMORIAL	163	429
WOMEN'S AUXILIARY AIR FORCE (WAAF)	119	345
WOMEN'S INSTITUTE	157	424a
WOMEN'S ROYAL ARMY CORPS	44	224
WOMEN'S ROYAL NAVAL SERVICE	147	417
WOMEN'S SECTION, THE ROYAL BRITISH LEGION	107	337
YANGTZE INCIDENT	132	405
THE 'Y' SERVICES MEMORIAL	33	212
YEOMANRY AVENUE	129	401
YMCA	158	424a
YORKSHIRE REGIMENT	75	311c

NATIONAL MEMORIAL ARBORETUM

Where our Nation remembers

All information in this Guidebook was accurate at time of print. ❦

Design by oceanbarefoot ❦

The Arboretum would like to give special thanks to everyone who contributed their photographs to this Guidebook. ❦
In particular, we thank Sue Elliott, David Faul, Fotocapricorn - Mike Twigg, David McDonnell, Nick Mott, Phil Nixon and Barry Turner. ❦